Becoming a
Millionaire
God's Way

Becoming a
Millionaire
God's Way

Getting Money to You, Not from You

DR. C. THOMAS ANDERSON

FOREWORD BY
ROBERT T. KIYOSAKI

Expanded Edition

New York Boston Nashville

FaithWords
Hachette Book Group USA
237 Park Avenue
New York, NY 10017

Visit our Web site at www.faithwords.com.

This FaithWords edition is published by arrangement with Winword Publishing, Inc., 3520 E. Brown Road, Mesa, AZ 85213.

Printed in the United States of America

First Hachette Book Group USA Edition: November 2006
Expanded Edition: September 2008
10 9 8 7 6 5 4 3 2 1

FaithWords is a division of Hachette Book Group USA, Inc.
The FaithWords name and logo are trademarks of Hachette Book Group USA, Inc.

Designed by Meryl Sussman Levavi

Library of Congress Cataloging-in-Publication Data

Anderson, C. Thomas (Carl Thomas), 1944–
    Becoming a millionaire God's way : getting money to you, not from you / C. Thomas Anderson ; foreword by Robert T. Kiyosaki. — Expanded ed.
        p. cm.
    ISBN-13: 978-0-446-51096-7
    ISBN-10: 0-446-51096-3
    1. Finance, Personal—Religious aspects. 2. Money—Religious aspects. I. Title.
    HG179.A55967 2008
    332.024'01—22

                                                          2008013693

Contents

Foreword

I DID NOT LIKE THE CHURCH MY FAMILY ATTENDED. THOUGH THE minister and congregation were very nice, there was always an underlying feeling that money and the desiring of money were evil. If you wanted to be rich and financially free, you were made to feel guilty for those feelings. I wanted to be rich and I began to feel very guilty. I had no problem with the other teachings of the church, but I simply could not accept that imposed guilt about money and the love of money.

My poor dad tended to agree with our church's point of view on money; maybe that is why he did not mind being a member of that church. My rich dad did not go to the same church; he taught me a different point of view about money and God. He said, "Money is not evil, but being a slave to money is. Due to lack of financial education at home, school, and church, most people become slaves to money, allowing it to dictate the limits of their lives, but a little financial education could make you a master of money."

Rich dad did not believe money had the power to cause people to become evil either:

Money does not corrupt you. Money only reveals to you who you really are. If you are greedy at the core, more money will only make you greedier. If you are cheap, more money will only make you cheaper. If you are a crook, more money will only make you more of a crook. If you are generous, more money will only make you more generous. If you are poor, more money will only make you poorer (which is why most lottery winners are soon broke). If you are a fool, more money will only make you a bigger fool. And if you are a master of money, your money will grow and prosper yourself as well as those around you because your money is doing God's work.

So rather than growing up feeling guilty about my desire to be wealthy, I learned from my rich dad how to be a master of money and how to use both my labor and my money to do God's work. Today, I continue to be friends with the families that attended my family church . . . the church I did not like. I notice that many of my friends continue to experience that same feeling of guilt, and also a fear that the desire for great wealth will corrupt them. Instead of learning to be masters of money, most seem to have become slaves to money—they work hard yet are burdened with debt, and they let money tell them what they can and cannot afford.

A mother of a friend I went to Sunday school with even said to me, "Robert, we are not like you. We did not sell our souls for money." She went on to say their souls were purer than mine because they had not given in to the temptations money brings. Needless to say, it hurt to be condemned for becoming rich.

My rich dad taught me differently. Many times we talked about the fact that you can become rich without selling your soul. In fact, if the truth be known, there are more poor and middle-class people who sell their souls for money; they work at jobs that kill their spirit, and they never become rich. "Money is just money," he would say. "Money in itself is not good or evil. It is how we acquire our money and what we do with it that reflects back to us if we are good, evil, greedy, crooked, foolish, ignorant, or masters of money. And yet it is very possible to become rich doing God's work. Many people do become rich in that way, and they never sell their souls. Just because a person is rich does not mean they are evil, crooked, or greedy."

After *Rich Dad, Poor Dad* was published, I was completely surprised by the number of church and religious leaders who thanked me for my book. I was even more surprised to hear that a few preachers were actually quoting from my book during their sermons! I began to realize how much I had been affected by those religious teachings of my youth, even though I thought I wasn't. I still felt guilty. I still believed the myth that all churches are against people becoming wealthy. I had carried that guilt for years. My eyes were closed and I did not see the other religious leaders who were teaching people to be masters or good stewards of money rather than declaring money to be evil in and of itself.

Because of religious leaders like Tom Anderson, my eyes are open at last. I now realize there are rich preachers and poor preachers, rich churches and poor churches.

Reverend Tom Anderson was one of the first religious leaders to contact me after my book came out. He is also the first preacher to ever ask me to speak to his church. I doubt if my church back in Hawaii would ever ask me to speak because my message about God and money would probably not fit theirs. So it is an honor to write this foreword for Reverend Tom's book. I did not choose to write this foreword because Reverend Tom uses my book or asked me to speak to his church. I write this foreword because of who Tom Anderson really is. I would never endorse a book written by someone who was not real. But Reverend Tom is real, and Reverend Tom practices what he preaches. In today's world, that is rare.

Tom Anderson is a master of money who teaches his congregation how to be the same. He is spiritually and financially a rich and generous person. He does not condemn others for being rich. He does not blind people to the power of money. He does not keep people ignorant about the power of money with feelings of guilt. He does not encourage his flock to be cheap—instead he commends them to be generous. Instead of condemning money, he teaches people to use the power of money in their favor, not against them. When it comes to money, Reverend Tom Anderson walks his talk and practices what he preaches . . . and that is the highest acknowledgment I can give anyone.

ROBERT T. KIYOSAKI

Introduction

MANY ARE TEACHING PEOPLE THAT THEY ARE TO PROSPER, BUT NO one is teaching them how. I was on my way to Dallas and, as I often do, I was using the time to study and pray. As often happens on such trips, God spoke to me. He told me to teach this series and write this book.

It began during a visit to the airport gift shop. I picked up *Rich Dad, Poor Dad*, a book by Robert T. Kiyosaki that dramatically changed my thinking about money. I read the book in its entirety during the flight, and its contents stayed on my mind as I prayed.

Mr. Kiyosaki wrote very candidly about the different perceptions between his two dads. His "poor" dad was his real father, who raised him with the traditional American views of success. He had a good salary, a nice house, and good benefits. He worked hard all his life for the money he made but was always heavily in debt and never really had anything extra. Mr. Kiyosaki's "rich" dad was actually his best friend's father who mentored him in the process of investing and gaining wealth. He did this by helping Robert learn how the rich look at money.

What gripped my attention most was the way Mr. Kiyosaki emphasized the fact that gaining wealth is not a matter of getting a good raise or a better job—it starts with learning a different way of looking at money. It involves a drastic change of perception, a whole new outlook on business and investment. It is this difference in perception that sets the wealthy apart from the poor.

Rich Dad, Poor Dad is not labeled a "Christian" book, but it is filled with biblical principles. I am indebted to Mr. Kiyosaki for his inspiration. I believe he wrote by God's direction for such a time as this. His book opened a whole new approach in my thinking, readying me for what was to come, so that when God spoke to me on that flight from Dallas, I was listening.

I realized that if the average person has such a mistaken view of wealth, how much more so does the average Christian, who not only doesn't understand how investment works, but actually believes God wants his people to stay poor? No wonder so many Christians are broke! No wonder God said to me, "No one is teaching them how to prosper."

The words hit hard. I am a prosperity preacher, and a big part of my twenty-year ministry has focused on teaching people that God never wants His people to be poor or sick or helpless. I am not just preaching prosperity either—I am living it.

That wasn't always the case, you understand. I grew up dirt poor. I experienced poverty firsthand. A spirit of poverty had been handed down from generation to generation. My father was a good man who worked hard all his life, but he was poor. He remodeled homes. He had two cabins that he rented. He fixed shoes. He sold ice. He was a school custodian and also drove a school bus. He worked hard all his life, but when he died, his total estate was worth only ten thousand dollars—to be split evenly between the four grandchildren. He had nothing to show for a life of hard work.

I was set up at an early age to do exactly what he did. At five years old, I worked alongside him. I learned a good work ethic and understood the principle of hard work early on. The Bible teaches that man was created to work. Before there was sin, Adam was told to tend the garden, to work. Proverbs 10:4 describes the diligent and the lazy: "He who has a slack hand becomes poor, but the hand of the diligent makes rich." A few chapters later, we are told "The soul of a lazy man desires, and has nothing; but the soul of the diligent shall be made rich" (Prov. 13:4). Hard work is a good thing; no one can really know satisfaction in life without it, but I also learned a poverty mentality. I grew up working hard to have just enough to get

> Poverty is a belief of the heart, not a condition of being without money.

by and then die with nearly nothing, just like my father and his father and his father. It is the way the world works. As God began to work in my life, I realized that working hard is not enough. Poverty is a belief of the heart, not a condition of being without money. I had poverty because I believed the world system that said I would have just enough to get by. Over the years, God changed my belief system and taught me to not only work hard, but also smart.

I will share many of those lessons later in this book. The first one, however, was really the most important, to change how I thought. To begin with, my wife, Maureen, and I applied the power of the Word. We were poor. Struggling. Trying to get by, day by day. Then we heard the prosperity message, that God wanted us prosperous. We began to do something about it.

Because the only thing that really changes anyone is the Word of God, we opened our ears to the message. Maureen made a tape with all the prosperity Scriptures on it. We played the tape continuously, twenty-four hours a day, in our house and in our car, and even as we slept. It played next to my ear all night long. We heard nothing but prosperity, prosperity, prosperity. Maureen made additional tapes with her voice and I made other tapes with my voice because we believe our own voice before we believe others.

As my heart changed, the poverty mentality left me. We began to experience God's abundance. For many years now, we have preached this message. It is a good message. The body of Christ has believed for too long that God is against wealth, that He wants us to be poor. We have told ourselves that somehow money is not spiritual, that it is instead filthy lucre, the root of all evil. When we get sick we console ourselves with the belief that God is teaching us patience, that He is using our infirmity to glorify Himself as we suffer for Him.

Yet there is nothing biblical about this kind of thinking. The truth is that when we are poor and sick it is because we think poor, we eat poor, and we live poor, not because God wants us that way. We have failed to overcome our own bad habits. We have failed to overcome the past. We have failed to overcome the resistance of the enemy. In short, we have failed to walk in faith. We have tried to justify our failure by convincing ourselves that our suffering is spiritual, and even God's will.

It is to our own detriment that we don't take any responsibility for these shortcomings. Neither do we make the effort required to change our thinking. We just continue to suffer and try to find some way of feeling good about it. Changing such thinking is one of the greatest challenges I face as a pastor. Yet until people think differently, they will continue to be poor and sick.

Unfortunately, the prosperity message doesn't quite go far enough, despite its relevance. Yes, we have taught people to tithe, and we have taught them about giving. We have taught them that God can miraculously provide for their needs. Yet there is an aspect of God's blessing we have ignored: We have not taught people the process of becoming

> We have taught them that they should be wealthy, but we have not taught them how.

wealthy. We have taught them that they should be wealthy, but we have not taught them how. It is time to take the next step.

When Israel left Egypt God sent manna to His people every morning. They always had enough for that day . . . all they had to do was pick it up! But God provided only enough for the day; there was never any left over. If the Israelites tried to store more than they needed, the manna spoiled overnight. They could never get ahead.

Abundance, the life of great blessing, was in the Promised Land. That was where Israel wanted to go, but it took forty years for God's people to get there. The reason it took so long was because they had to learn how to think differently. In Egypt they were slaves who had nothing and never expected to get more than nothing. They were slaves and that was as much as slaves could expect. That's how the system worked.

In the wilderness they had to rid themselves of their slave mentality, their poverty mentality. God's people had to learn to rely entirely on Him and His Word. Only when they knew His ability to meet their every need were the Israelites ready to enter the land of abundance—the land promised them. Though they had seen miracles in the wilderness and their needs were met, there was nothing extra. By the time they took hold of the promises of God and entered the Promised Land, they were no longer slaves. They were conquerors who drove out the giants in residence! They thought differently.

An interesting thing happened when Israel entered the Promised Land, however. The miraculous provision of God stopped as soon as they ate of the fat of the land: "Then the manna ceased on the day after they had eaten the produce of the land; and the children of Israel no longer had manna, but they ate the food of the land of Canaan that year" (Jos. 5:12). The manna stopped coming. The people could no longer walk out in the morning and pick up their food for the day. That year the people ate the produce of the land; they moved into abundance. Though they now had to work for what they got, had to plow the ground and plant seeds and harvest crops, at last they could get ahead and have more than just enough for the day.

But with abundance came a need to learn how to produce wealth. God blessed their work, but they had to work, and not just hard but also smart. They had to know some things. The Promised Land flowed with milk and honey, but to get milk from a cow, they had to know how to milk a cow and they had to have the self-discipline to actually go out and milk it every day. To get honey, they had to learn something about bees. God's people too often think that all they have to do is confess prosperity and wait for it to come. God said He would teach us how to produce wealth, and that He will bless our efforts, but we still have to do something to produce it (Deut. 29:9; 30:9; and James 2:17).

> God blessed their work, but they had to work, and not just hard but also smart.

What God was saying to me that day on the flight to Dallas was that it is time for the body of Christ to take the next step. Many have come out of the poverty of Egypt and entered the wilderness and begun to learn of God's miraculous provision. There are testimonies of God changing impossible situations and providing for needs when it was impossible. Many in the body have learned to rely on Him completely. They have learned to tithe and to give and to expect God to meet their every need—yet they only have enough for the day. The time has come to learn how to make money enough for the future as well as today.

God is not going to drop abundance out of heaven. That only happens in the wilderness . . . and it is never more than what is needed that day. He's not going to counterfeit money for you either. And you can't pray for someone else to change so they will just give you money—that is wilderness thinking. To enter abundance you have to change. You have to learn the attributes, qualities, and skills to become wealthy. For the promises of God to be effective in your life, changes need to happen inside of you. *Rich Dad, Poor Dad* addressed the difference in perception between the rich and the poor. *Becoming a Millionaire God's Way* addresses the same problem of perception as it relates to the church.

> To enter abundance you have to change. You have to learn the attributes, qualities, and skills to become wealthy.

You were made in the image of God (Gen. 1:26–27). If you believe God wants you to be poor, then you are saying you are a reflection of the image of a god who must also be poor. So while you may believe He owns all the cattle on a thousand hills, you also maintain that He doesn't want His people to share in that wealth. Such perceptions must be those of a poor god. If God is that poor, then it is hard to have much faith in Him. If your perception of God is that He is rich, then you should be rich just as He is. Our perceptions need to change so that they are more like God's. And His perceptions are not poor (Rev. 3:18).

Consider our giving. The tithe is that part of our income that belongs to God. When we give it back to Him, we protect everything else we own (Mal. 3:11). It's like an insurance policy. An offering is anything above and beyond the tithe. It is this, the offering, that the Word calls seed. We plant seed in the kingdom of God by giving more than the tithe God requires. It is this seed that produces thirty, sixty, and a hundredfold. Unfortunately, we have not seen that the offering is seed planted in the spiritual world. Seed always produces after its own kind; the benefit of an offering is a spiritual blessing.

Yet for an offering to have any effect on our material wealth, we must also plant seed in the material world—there must be some kind of investment. The spiritual blessing of an offering will multiply the material seed of an investment, yet if there is no investment there is nothing to multiply. Money, a material thing, will not rain out of the heavens as a spiritual blessing. Offerings are an important part of the process, but they must be linked to seed planted somewhere in the world.

As God spoke this message to me, He gave me these chapters that were transformed into an extensive series of teachings. My goal in relating these teachings to you is to help you take the next step. Having picked up this book, you are probably already convinced that God wants you to prosper; you just haven't figured out how.

That's what we're going to learn over the next fourteen chapters. We will start by figuring out where you are at now. We will then take steps to develop an enthusiasm and passion for becoming financially literate. We will study how to change bad attitudes and habits. Together we will look at ways to find money to invest. And finally, we will talk about the process of investment. God delivered me from a poverty mentality. In the years since that deliverance, I have been blessed to learn increasingly more about money, both from my own experience and that of others. With a greater sense of financial literacy has come a desire to share what I know. May all who are ready to enter God's abundance read and learn what they need to know, and may they too reach the place God wants them to be.

Becoming a
Millionaire
God's Way

1

Get a Grip

THE FIRST STEP IN ACHIEVING WEALTH IS TO ANSWER A SIMPLE QUES-tion: "Where am I right now?"

This task may prove a little disconcerting, but it is important for two reasons. First of all, most people are nowhere near arriving at the financial position they ought to be in. Don't be concerned about this fact, but be aware. Don't throw up your hands in despair and give up; instead, let this reality inspire you to make some changes. Be concerned in the sense that you know you have some work to do—which means bringing your finances under control so you can do something with them.

Second, and more important, if you don't know where you are, then you don't know where you need to start. Most people don't even know how much money they have in their checkbook, much less where it is going. Many don't even know how to balance their checkbook. Find out where you are starting from.

To begin this process you need to establish your net worth. This is a simple matter of listing all of your assets and how much they are worth. If you converted everything you own into cash, how much would you have?

2 ~ Dr. C. Thomas Anderson

You must be very objective in this task in order to assemble an accurate picture. An inflated and unrealistic appraisal of your assets will probably make you feel good about yourself, but it won't help you reach the goal of becoming wealthy. Be objective and realistic.

For example, if you bought a refrigerator for $1,000 one month ago, you cannot count it as a $1,000 asset today. If you try to sell it you might only get $300 for it, so in reality it is a $300 dollar asset. If you are making payments on it and still owe $500, then it does not even count as an asset.

Determine how much equity you have in your house, your furniture, your car, everything you own. When you add all the figures together, this is your net worth.

Now determine what your net worth should be at this point in your life. Take your taxable income for the last year and multiply it by your age. (If computing these numbers for a husband and wife together, use either person's age, but you will be better using the older one.) Divide that number by ten and you will have the amount your net worth should be at this point in your life. By subtracting your actual net worth you can see how far off you are.

If you are like most people, the resulting figure will be far below your potential. Though some are starting at this figure, most are behind. And even if you are behind, you now have a goal to work toward. This number of what amount should be your net worth is only a guideline, however; don't let it become a limit. There is no reason you can't achieve hundreds of times that amount.

The next question to consider: "Now that I know where I am, how did I get here?" This is the focus of the rest of the chapter. It is not an accident of fate that you are where you are. Your current financial picture is the result of a combination of decisions you have made in the past. If you do not change the choices you made in the past, you will end up in the same place in the future. If you are not satisfied with where you are, then you must change some things or the same patterns will continue and you will remain in the same place in the future. Proverbs 23:7 says it very simply: "For as he thinks in his heart, so is he." Ultimately your thoughts from yesterday put you where you are today. If you are in poverty today it is

> If you want to be a millionaire tomorrow, you must start thinking like a millionaire today.

because you thought and accepted poverty yesterday. If you want to be a millionaire tomorrow, you must start thinking like a millionaire today.

How does a millionaire think? A millionaire who loses all his money will begin immediately to look for ways to make it all back again. His first thought is of where he can invest. A millionaire who goes broke today will earn it back many times over. We hear about the one who lost all his money in the stock market and jumped out of a window, but we don't hear about the dozens, even hundreds, who make it all back the next day or the next week. A millionaire thinks of how much he will make, not how much he lost.

Home Environment

Knowing where you came from will help you make necessary changes. The bad thought patterns you have today are really habitual. Though you have had them for so long that you may think of them as natural, you weren't born with them. You learned them somewhere, mainly from your parents, your family, and your experiences. Those patterns of thinking began in childhood and have influenced your life choices and even the kind of work you have looked for.

For our study, we will identify six types of childhood homes or home environments that have affected many people adversely. Most of us can find our own experience within one of these descriptions.

Controlling

If you grew up in a controlling home, you were probably not allowed to do much for yourself. Controlling parents won't let children dress themselves, feed themselves, or choose activities for themselves. By the time such children are in school they often can't tie their own shoes or even butter their own bread. As children they never learned to take on responsibility, and as adults they generally feel they can't. Such people will shirk responsibility for the rest of their lives. They can't make decisions because they were never allowed to make decisions. Children of controlling homes avoid any kind of job that carries much responsibility with it. They will believe and will say, "I can't do it. I don't know how."

Parents who are controlling in this way usually gain a sense of self-value by making children feel like they are doing something useful and self-sacrificing by taking care of them. Unfortunately, these parents also limit their children's ability to take on the kind of responsibility necessary to excel in life.

Fear-Based

A similar type of home is grounded in fear. Children who grow up in fear generally have no motivation. They are afraid to do anything or try anything that might result in failure. They don't make decisions because they are afraid of making the wrong decision.

> Children who grow up in fear generally have no motivation.

Children need to learn responsibility for themselves at an early age. We have two sons, Scot and Jason. By the time they were two and three months old, I was standing them up and holding them so they could do leg lifts and strengthen their muscles. By the time they were seven months old, they were already walking. At two years old, they were tying their own shoes and dressing themselves. Sometimes the clothes were on backwards and their shoes were on the wrong feet, but they were trained to take on the challenge without fear. At an early age they were responsible for themselves.

We never had a problem getting them to go to bed. We trained them to know that when it was bedtime, they went. They never argued. Even if we didn't tell them, when it was time, they went. We never had to get them up for school. They got up and went. We never had to get them up to go to college. They got up and went. We never had to get them up to go to work. They got up and went. Today Scot and Jason carry a great amount of responsibility. They virtually run Living Word Bible Church. They are not overwhelmed by their responsibilities; they are instead excited. They seek responsibility out. I'm not bragging. I'm giving you an example of how critical it is that children learn to be responsible for themselves at an early age. It has a tremendous impact on their future.

Insecure

A third type of childhood environment is the insecure home, which often occurs when there is divorce or separation. Money becomes a problem and the parents keep telling the kids over and over how bad things are. The children learn to worry about having enough, something that kids would probably not even notice if they weren't told repeatedly. By the time they are adults, they are constantly striving to gain a little security. If they can just get a few dollars in the bank, just make enough money to get by, just have a secure job that will give them a small retirement, they'll be okay. Their whole lives are spent trying to be secure—and never learning to take any risks. They are never able to operate in faith because they can't step out of that security and into what is likely to be both uncertain and unfamiliar.

Gaining great wealth requires taking some risks. As you become financially literate you will avoid taking foolish risks, but no investment is a sure thing. There is always some risk. Those who seek security find it very difficult to become truly wealthy.

Abusive

Some grew up in homes where there was abuse—physical, sexual, or emotional. The message perceived by the abused child is that he has no value. Such children often turn to drugs or alcohol or tobacco—anything that abuses their bodies. They rebel against social norms and have a very difficult time believing that they could ever amount to anything important enough to actually fit into society. They can't accumulate wealth because everything they gain is squandered in self-abuse, which deep down they believe they deserve. They just don't fit in.

Performance-Based

A fifth type of home is based on performance. You were loved only if you did your job well. Children raised in this environment are always trying to please their parents, their teachers, their employers . . . everybody. They make very good employees, but won't think for themselves and therefore must be given to-do lists. They always work very hard, but they never learn to respect those they are trying to please. They never learn to build. They also never take risks because they are afraid of failure. If they make an investment and it is not successful, they believe they won't be loved anymore.

Hyper-Responsible

A sixth problem is the home where children are given too much responsibility at an early age. We already talked about the importance of training children to take on responsibility for themselves. The problem comes when they are forced to become responsible for others at too early an age. For example, when there is a divorce, a son might become the man of the house at eight or ten years old. Or Mom is working all the time and one of the children (usually the oldest) has to take care of the younger siblings. In our society where the traditional nuclear family has become less common, this can be a very significant problem.

> You don't have to simply accept the direction your childhood pointed you toward.

These children grow up without their childhood. They mature too quickly and react in one of two ways: Either they spend their lives trying to be kids again or they become so overly responsible they can't take chances. They can't risk any kind of investment because it would be irresponsible in their minds.

You may have identified yourself in one of these categories. It is important to realize that you don't have to simply accept the direction your childhood pointed you toward. Now that you recognize the problem, you can deal with it. A lot of parents did a lot of damage to their kids, but you don't have to live out the damage. The Bible tells us to honor and love our parents, but we don't have to honor the junk they put in us. We can move on. In fact, we have to.

Overcoming the Past

The Bible is filled with accounts of great men and women of God who overcame bad upbringing. In Genesis 25–27 we see something of Jacob's childhood. He grew up in a home with considerable insecurity. His father clearly and openly loved his brother, Esau, more than him and gave Esau preferential treatment. His mom and dad argued religion all the time. She wanted the blessing to go to the younger son, the one God wanted. His dad was more hung up on tradition and wanted the blessing for the oldest son. Jacob and his mother had to deceive Isaac when he was old and blind and so sick he couldn't tell the difference between a hairy arm and a goat skin.

Jacob's own brother hated him so much he wanted to kill him. Jacob had to run for his life. It is hard to imagine a more unlikely candidate to achieve wealth. He would probably have been voted least likely to succeed by his graduating class. In his lowest moment, however, he made a promise to God.

> *Then Jacob made a vow, saying, "If God will be with me, and keep me in this way that I am going, and give me bread to eat and clothing to put on, so that I come back to my father's house in peace, then the Lord shall be my God. And this stone which I have set as a pillar shall be God's house, and of all that You give me I will surely give a tenth to You." (Gen. 28:20–22)*

Jacob promised he would start tithing. This was the beginning of change in him but for fourteen years, he didn't make a dime. He worked seven years for a wife and it was the wrong one. He worked another seven years for the other wife. He still didn't have any money to tithe on. He finally went to his father-in-law, Laban, who was also his employer, and complained.

> *Thus I have been in your house twenty years; I served you fourteen years for your two daughters, and six years for your flock, and you have changed my wages ten times. (Gen. 31:41)*

Many could make the same complaint about their employer. Your boss is ripping you off, paying you minimal wages while you make him wealthy. It is a common complaint. But somewhere along the way Jacob made a big change in his thinking. He began to work smarter. Back in chapter 30, we find him making a proposal to his boss.

And it came to pass, when Rachel had borne Joseph, that Jacob said to Laban, "Send me away, that I may go to my own place and to my country. Give me my wives and my children for whom I have served you, and let me go; for you know my service which I have done for you." (Gen. 30:25–26)

In other words, "I've been here all this time. I have nothing to show for it. I haven't experienced any blessing, haven't even had enough money to tithe. I'm tired of wasting my time. I want to get out of here."

In verse 28 Laban said, "Name me your wages, and I will give it." So Jacob got smart. He said to Laban, "Let me have all of the animals with blemishes on them. You don't want them anyway. You keep all the others." Jacob was no longer just working hard and he was not thinking anymore in the way that his early life taught him to think. He was thinking like a millionaire. Instead of seeking security and just getting by, he decided to do something, take a few chances, change some things—and God finally had something to bless. Jacob peeled some bark from tree branches and put it in front of the animal's watering troughs. God blessed Jacob's obedience and his efforts, and the flocks bore speckled and spotted young. Scripture makes it clear that his life changed: "Thus the man became exceedingly prosperous" (Gen. 30:43).

Jacob overcame his past by starting to think differently. He gained a new perspective on his life. Later he attributed the change to a dream.

And it happened, at the time when the flocks conceived, that I lifted my eyes and saw in a dream, and behold, the rams which leaped upon the flocks were streaked, speckled, and gray-spotted. Then the Angel of God spoke to me in a dream, saying, "Jacob." And I said, "Here I am." And He said, "Lift your eyes now and see, all the rams which leap on the flocks are streaked, speckled, and gray-spotted; for I have seen all that Laban is doing to you. I am the God of Bethel, where you anointed the pillar and where you made a vow to Me." (Gen. 31:10–13)

The pattern Jacob went through to become exceedingly wealthy is shown in these verses. First he committed himself to tithing and it is significant that, while this commitment did not make him wealthy overnight, it was at that moment that God took notice of his situation. God was working on him from that moment on. But he had a lot to overcome. For a while he worked hard but had nothing to show for it. Then he got hold of a new vision from God in a dream and, as a result, started thinking like a millionaire. He looked for ways to change his position and God blessed him because of it.

Many others in the Bible overcame their past in the same way. Moses was abandoned by his family, left to float away in a basket. He was driven out of Egypt as a murderer and lived for years on the back side of the wilderness. Joseph was sold into slavery by his own brothers. He spent years in prison because of the lies of a vindictive woman, even though he had done nothing wrong. Abraham, David, and Solomon all had stuff to get over. But they all did it. Paul said it this way:

Brethren, I do not count myself to have apprehended; but one thing I do, forgetting those things which are behind and reaching forward to those things which are ahead, I press toward the goal for the prize of the upward call of God in Christ Jesus. (Phil. 3:13–14)

In other words, to achieve real success, you have to leave behind abuse, unfair treatment you have endured, the insecurity, and fear. You must move on. Faith doesn't work in the past. You can't change the past. You can't even change the present. But you can change the future. However, you have to leave the past behind to get there. The biggest hindrance to wealth is our past.

Vision for the Future

Like Jacob we must get a vision of the future God wants for us. A vision is about being able to see what is possible and being unhindered by the past. It is the ability to look past the obvious and see opportunity.

Some of the richest men in the history of America started with nothing—John Rockefeller, J.C. Penney, Frank Woolworth, Del LeTourneau. They all share one thing in common with the wealthiest men of the Bible. They got a vision from God and left their past behind. Proverbs speaks about vision. The King James Version is most familiar to us—"Where there is no vision, the people perish" (Prov. 29:18).

> A vision is about being able to see what is possible and being unhindered by the past. It is the ability to look past the obvious and see opportunity.

In other words, without a vision for the future, without setting a purpose in your heart to pursue, you will go backwards and accomplish nothing. There are things you can do. No one is devoid of all skills or knowledge and no one is incapable of learning. Your mind is like a muscle. The more you use it the better it works. You just need a vision of where you are going so you can get started. You need to get a grip, not only on your finances but also on your thinking. Your first step to wealth is to think differently.

By this time many of you are thinking, "I don't really have a vision, other than a vague concept of becoming wealthy." You need to begin by looking at your strengths. As you seek God you will find that there are things you like to do, even love to do, because that's where your talent is. Find out what you love to do and learn to do it better than anyone else. When you do that, someone will be willing to pay you for it.

I found that I like to preach. I like to teach. I like being a pastor. Every day I set out to do it better than I did the day before. I want to be the best at it that I can be. And people pay me to do it.

Beyond that, there is a vision from the Word of God that we all need to have. It is in Proverbs 13:22. We have all heard the second part of that verse, "But the wealth of the sinner is stored up for the righteous." We get very excited about that but we need to recognize that it is only half of a two-part state-

> The goal for all of us should be to leave an inheritance.

ment. This verse is an example of a form of Hebrew poetry construction called antithetical parallelism. That means that it makes a statement in the first line and then contrasts it with its opposite. In simple terms, it makes a positive statement and follows it with a negative. The part we just read is the negative. The first half of Proverbs 13:22 is important for a complete understanding of the verse, which reads:

A good man leaves an inheritance to his children's children,
but the wealth of the sinner is stored up for the righteous.

In other words, the goal for all of us should be to leave an inheritance. If we are "good" and "righteous," then we will strive for that. If we do not strive for it, then our wealth will be given to others. Locating a vision to help you get a grip is a good place to start.

Chapter 1 Summary

Get a Grip

The first step in achieving wealth is to answer a simple question:

"Where am I right now?"

1. List all of your assets and what they are worth (house, furniture, car, etc.). Be conservative, not inflated, in your estimates. The total is your net worth.

"Where should I be now?"

1. Take your taxable income for the last year and multiply it by your age.
2. Divide the result by ten. The result is what your net worth should be.

Subtract your actual net worth from what your net worth should be, and you'll see how much work you have to do.

Keys to Making Changes

Our biggest hindrance to wealth is our past.

You got to the place you are now by the choices you made in the past. To improve your position, you need to make some changes. Think differently. Your thoughts from yesterday put you where you are today. If you want to be a millionaire tomorrow, you must start thinking like a millionaire today.

The bad habits that you have today were learned. They began with the environment of your home as a child. To be successful, you must overcome the past. Know where you came from. Does your childhood home fit one of the following categories?

1. Controlling: If you lived in a controlling home, you never learned to make decisions for yourself. You probably avoid anything that requires taking on much responsibility.
2. Fear-Based: Children who grow up in fear generally are afraid to try anything that might result in failure.
3. Insecure: Children learn to worry about having enough. They spend their lives trying to gain security and never learn to take risks.
4. Abusive: They have no self-worth, so they become self-abusive and squander everything they gain.
5. Performance-Based: They always try to please others. They never take risks because they are afraid that if they fail, they won't be loved.
6. Hyper-Responsible: Forced to become responsible for others at too early an age, they grow up without their childhood. They either spend their lives trying to be kids again, or they become so overly responsible they can't take risks.

Jacob grew up in an insecure home (Gen. 25:19–34; 27:1–28:9). He worked for an employer who took advantage of him (Gen. 29–30). He overcame by following these basic steps:

1. He committed himself to tithing (Gen. 28:22).
2. He got a new vision and started thinking in terms of prosperity.
3. He changed his thinking and started to work smarter.
4. He took some chances instead of seeking security.

God blessed his efforts and multiplied his possessions.

Get a Vision

A vision is about being able to see what is possible and being unhindered by the past. It is the ability to look past the obvious and see opportunity.

Begin by looking at your strengths. When you do what you love to do and are good at, someone will pay you for it.

Attitude Determines Altitude

ONE DAY A MAN WALKED BY A LITTLE CHINESE tattoo shop and happened to notice a customer in the middle of having "Born to Lose" tattooed on his arm. Curious, he waited until the operation was completed and the man left. Seeking out the owner of the shop he asked, "Why would anyone ever get 'Born to Lose' tattooed on his arm?"

The Chinese man looked at him and said, "Tattoo in heart before on arm."

It is a fact of life that what is in the heart will eventually come out. We all love to put on a good front for people to see but it is only a front. The attitude hidden behind it will bear fruit and it will limit your potential. Your attitude will determine your altitude. You will never achieve or succeed in life higher than your attitude.

Consider these thoughts about attitudes. Attitude has its roots in words and its fruit in actions. The things we speak not only reflect our attitude but they also help mold our attitude. Sooner or later the attitude will erupt in action. Your behavior is directly connected to what you believe in your heart. If you have a good attitude, you will have good action. If you have a bad attitude, you will have bad action. What you believe in your heart produces the action of your hands, and what you believe is directly reflected in your attitude. What you believe is your attitude.

Attitudes are never content until they are expressed. You can hide them for a while but they will find a way out. You can't just ignore them. You have to change them. Your attitude will take you where you want to go or it will keep you where you are. When you meet someone and they are introduced with the phrase, "This is George. He's an investor," you immediately have a different perception of him. You think of wealth because an investor must be wealthy. Why then do we continue to struggle, instead of learning to become an investor? A right attitude will inspire us to break out of the mold we have been in and try something new.

Attitude is your best friend or your worst enemy. Which one it becomes will largely depend on the choices you make. You can't blame outside circumstances. A bad attitude might seem to be justified, given the way you have been treated or the hardships you've had to endure, but it is still a bad attitude and it will affect your future. Change it before it does. Your attitude will draw people to you or it will drive them away.

> Attitude is your best friend or your worst enemy. Which one it becomes will largely depend on the choices you make.

Attitude is the library of your past, the speaker of your present, and the prophet of your future. Your attitude tells much about your past experiences. It also indicates where you are right now and gives a good indication of where you will end up if you don't change it now. Attitude is also a measure of maturity. When you finally realize you are responsible for your attitude, you have grown up at last.

If you condensed the Bible to its most basic essence, you would find one resounding theme: God is interested in the thoughts, attitudes, and intentions of the heart. All of creation, with the exception of Noah and his family and the animals in the Ark, was destroyed because the world had become so wicked that every thought and attitude was continually evil. God cares about attitudes. It's not that we don't have justification for bad attitudes. We often do. That's not the point. It's just that the bad attitude will keep you from getting to where you want to be, no matter how justifiable it is.

Joseph certainly had ample reason to develop a bad attitude. His brothers hated him. That alone is enough for most of us. "My family doesn't like me. Life is tough. I have really low self-esteem." In Joseph's case they hated him so much they threw him into a pit and sold him into slavery. He ended up in Potiphar's house where, because of his good attitude, he was given charge of virtually everything.

Yet Potiphar's wife accused him of attempted rape and in no time he was in prison. He certainly would have been justified in having a bad attitude after that. It seemed that he was just cursed. But instead, he ended up running the jail.

He had an opportunity to get out when he interpreted the dream of the cupbearer who promised to mention his plight to Pharaoh. But once the cupbearer was free, he forgot about Joseph for two full years. He could have felt very abandoned at that point and developed a perfectly justified bad attitude. But he didn't and ultimately God not only freed him from prison but made him one of the most powerful men in the world, the source of salvation for his own family and for the entire nation.

If Joseph had reason for a bad attitude, then Jesus had even more. He never did anything wrong, yet all kinds of people hated him and tried to kill him. Yet he was happy. He expected good in all circumstances. He was confident. He was forgiving. He was compassionate. He was content. He was motivated. He was a peacemaker. In trouble he drew closer to God rather than blaming Him. He was diligent, focused, and flexible. He was not a legalist. He was pure in heart. He was a helper. He was full of mercy. The attitude Jesus demonstrated was never dependent on outside circumstances. He chose to have a good attitude. Without it He could never have fulfilled His mission in life.

The Right Attitude

A good attitude is absolutely essential for a good life. Knowing that, we should look closely at our attitudes toward money. What do we really believe concerning money? We seem to know that we can't get by without it, yet we have been told our whole lives that it is the root of all evil. It is really not surprising that Christians have such a difficult time with it. We want to be spiritual

> A good attitude is absolutely essential for a good life.

and not bothered with all this worldly stuff, yet we can't seem to find any other practical way to live. Let's examine, then, our attitudes concerning wealth. Ask yourself the question, "How important is money?" Your answer will say a lot about your attitudes.

The tendency has always been to say it is not important at all. We love the nobility of declaring, "I don't do it for the money." It sounds so much more godly and spiritual that way. "You can't serve God and Mammon." "It's all filthy lucre." The odds are we don't know what Mammon and lucre even are, but we know they must be awful. The moment our paycheck is short a couple of dollars, however, the superficiality of that kind of thinking comes blatantly to the forefront. We get upset. We complain about the stupidity of the payroll department. We attack our boss. We tell everyone who will listen so that they will know we have been wronged.

The contrast is interesting. The average person may claim that money doesn't matter much, yet he still works very hard for money. He knows that without it he can't have a house, a car, clothes, or even food. He devotes tremendous effort to obtaining it and tremendous worry to not having enough of it. His real attitude is manifested in his actions.

"Ah, " you might say, "but in the ministry, things are supposed to be more spiritual. Money doesn't matter there." I don't think the electric company would agree if the church refused to pay its bill. The church building costs money. The furniture in the building costs money. It costs money to turn the lights on. You cannot even pass out tracts and witness to people on the street if someone doesn't pay for the tract. Missionaries need money. Ministries need money. The work of the church simply cannot happen without money.

How important is money? It is extremely important. If we try to say that it is not, then our attitude is shallow at best and in most cases downright hypocritical. We need a new attitude.

Why is it so important? A few years ago, Peter Daniels, one of the wealthiest men in the world, conducted a seminar here at Living Word Bible Church. He spent several days teaching about how to gain wealth. One afternoon, between sessions, one of our staff spoke with a young man in the congregation and asked him how he was enjoying the seminar. With a tone of superiority in his voice, he explained that he had not been to any of the meetings, because he was not interested in money. That wasn't where God was leading him.

Exactly twenty-four hours later he was back at the church, tears in his eyes, asking if the church could help with some money for his neighbor. A fire had destroyed everything she owned and she was left destitute with several children to care for. Suddenly money mattered. If this young man had seen the importance of money in ministry somewhat earlier in his life, he might have been in a better position to minister to his neighbor without having to ask someone else for the support, without having to depend on others who did care about money.

Our attitude toward money has left us unable to really participate in effective ministry. We have to get over the attitude that money is bad. In fact, the Bible never says that. First Timothy 6:10 says the love of money is a root of all kinds of evil, not the money itself. If you love money, then you have a wrong attitude, but if you desire money so that you can do all of the things God has called you to do, then you have your priorities right. God wants to bless you. If you think this book is designed to get you rich just so you can sit back and be comfortable, then you have missed the point, but recognize that God would love to have you enjoy your wealth. He just doesn't want it to control you. He wants your attitude to be right.

Understanding Tithes and Offerings

In the introduction, I alluded to a concept I want to explain in more detail. I was introduced to this understanding of history by a good friend, Del LeTourneau, whose insights have been valuable in producing this book. He shared this with me during a recent golf game.

Through most of history, society has been very rural and agricultural. Virtually everyone worked on farms or in jobs associated with the products of farming. When Jesus spoke parables about sowing seed, everyone understood Him perfectly. He taught about sowing seed into the ground that had the potential to produce a hundred seeds from the one. Depending on the weather and the condition of the soil and how well it was cared for, it might only produce thirty or sixty times but everyone listening to Him understood the potential of a seed to multiply. A seed produces more seed after its own kind. If a farmer plants one sack of seed he can expect to harvest one hundred sacks.

A farmer in biblical times always knew he had to do certain things with the harvest in order to insure another harvest the next year. First, he took the tithe, the first tenth, the first fruits, into the storehouse, which in Old Testament times was the Temple, and he gave it to the Lord. This was his insurance that God would protect everything else that he owned. The tithe was the only thing God required of him.

Next, he might also choose to give an offering. By doing so, he would be planting seed in the kingdom of God. He could give any amount over the tithe. God didn't specify any exact percentage for an offering. This seed would produce a spiritual blessing that would cause multiplication. The tithe was never intended to be seed sown in the kingdom of God. The offering served that purpose.

The same principle holds true for our giving. Our tithe is that which belongs to God in the first place. It is not seed. When we give it, we protect all of the rest of our possessions. On the basis of the tithe, God rebukes the enemy for us so that he cannot touch anything that belongs to us (Mal. 3:11). The tithe is an insurance policy.

When we choose to give an offering above and beyond our tithe, we are planting seed that has the capacity to multiply thirty, sixty, or a hundredfold. The problem is in our expectation of what happens after that. We have heard the message "Money Cometh." We believe the windows of heaven are going to be opened and that God is going to pour out a blessing so great it cannot be contained. We have the Scripture to back up that belief.

Unfortunately, the blessing that is poured out is a blessing that multiplies the seed we have planted somewhere in the world. The farmer knew the tithe and the offering he took to the Temple would not produce anything directly. He could not come back to the Temple in a few months and collect a harvest. The tithe protected his stuff and the offering produced a spiritual multiplication but if he did not plant something in the ground, there would be nothing to multiply. One hundred times zero is still zero.

After the tithe and offering, all of the rest of the seed was available for the farmer to eat. But if he ate the rest of it, there would be no harvest next year. Therefore, in addition to the tithe and the offering, he always kept another bag of seed out of the harvest to plant in the ground. The tithe went to the storehouse. The offering was planted in the kingdom of God. The other seed was planted in the ground. In a way, the offering was a spiritual seed and the planting was a material seed. But they were linked together. The spiritual offering resulted in a multiplication of the seed in the ground. To be successful, he needed both.

> The tithe went to the storehouse. The offering was planted in the kingdom of God.

When we give an offering today, it produces a spiritual blessing on everything we touch. But if we have not planted anything in the ground, if we have not invested anything anywhere, there is nothing for the blessing to affect. We have to give God something to work with. Malachi 3, where the promises to open the windows of heaven are given, talks about blessing on things planted in the ground—crops, vines, and fruit—not the things brought into the Temple or the storehouse.

As history moved into the industrial age, many of our attitudes began to change. We started getting paychecks instead of seed. We learned to spend every penny. We charged and spent until we often could barely get a tithe in. In fact, most people have to fudge a little and even skip the tithe on occasion because there just isn't enough money left at the end of the week. Occasionally we get an offering in but we rarely even think seriously about saving some of our seed, our paycheck, to make an investment.

As a result, even when we have a spiritual blessing, there is really nothing planted in the ground that God can multiply for us. We wonder why we don't see the abundance that the Word talks about but we have eaten most of our seed instead of planting it in the ground.

When Jesus told the parable of the ten minas, He was demonstrating an attitude toward money. The story is found in Luke 19:11–27. A man went to a distant country to be made king. He called ten of his servants in and gave them each one mina to invest while he was gone. A mina was a measure of money equal to about three months' wages for the average person. The king gave them very specific instructions in verse 13 about what to do with it: "Do business till I come." The New International Version phrases it this way: "'Put this money to work,' he said, 'until I come back.'"

While the king was gone, some of his servants sent word that they did not want him to be their king. But he became the king anyway. When he came back he called his servants in to see what they had done with the money he had given them.

Two out of the ten had invested their money and multiplied it. The first increased the total to ten. The second had five. In both cases the king showed that he approved by his words to them: "Well done, good and faithful servant." It is interesting to note that this is the only place Jesus ever says these words, in a context dealing with the handling of money.

His reaction to the third servant was markedly different. This man brought back the mina he had been given and explained what he had done with it, or rather, what he had not done:

Then another came, saying, "Master, here is your mina, which I have kept put away in a handkerchief. For I feared you, because you are an austere man. You collect what you did not deposit, and reap what you did not sow." (Luk. 19:20–21)

In other words, the third servant operated out of fear and insecurity. He did nothing with the money. His attitude was to play it completely safe and not lose anything. He neither took risks nor made investments. His king was disappointed in him, to say the least.

And he said to him, "Out of your own mouth I will judge you, you
wicked servant. You knew that I was an austere man, collecting
what I did not deposit and reaping what I did not sow. Why then
did you not put my money in the bank, that at my coming I might
have collected it with interest?" (Luk. 19:22–23)

The servant who was afraid to take chances and make investments was considered a wicked servant. In verse 24 the king
showed his displeasure even more: "Take the *mina* from him, and
give it to him who has ten *minas*."

It was worse still for the other seven servants. They didn't
even bring the one *mina* back. Apparently they just spent it.
They are probably the ones who the king refers to as not want-
ing him to even be their king. They ate their seed and, rather
than face their master, they preferred to rebel against him. Their
fate was the worst of all: "But bring here those enemies of mine,
who did not want me to reign over them, and slay them before
me" (Luk. 19:27).

Another verse we are familiar with is in 2 Timothy—"Be diligent to present yourself approved to God, a worker who does not
need to be ashamed, rightly dividing the word of truth" (2:15).
We usually look at this verse and say that we need to study the
Bible more so that God will approve of us. But there are some
words here that we need to look at a little more closely. First of
all, note the word "diligent." It means to work hard and faithfully
at something, to be diligent and intense. Another word in this
same line is "worker." This verse has something to do with intense
and consistent effort.

The word "truth" in this context is very easy to miss. It doesn't
actually mean the Bible. It refers rather to that which is true in
the Bible, a subtle distinction but an important one. "Approved"
actually means to use your mind, to have been thinking. To come
before the Lord approved means to come with proper preparation and thought.

Among the ten servants discussed above, the ones who came before the king approved were the first two. They were the ones who had taken the time to diligently work, think, and prepare for the return of the king by doing what he had told them to do, which was to put the money to work. They took what they had and they multiplied it. Thus they were approved as "good and faithful servants."

This parable has many applications, but all of them point to the fact that Jesus left this earth to become king and He expects His servants to deal wisely with the material things of this world while He is gone. It's the same message as Proverbs 13:22. A righteous man builds an inheritance. It's difficult to get around the idea that God intends His people to have an interest in money.

Thinking Like a Millionaire

There is a distinct difference between the attitude of the wealthy toward money and the attitude of the average person. Here are some keys to understanding how the wealthy think:

The Average Person Works for Money

The wealthy make money work for them. We have already talked about how desperate we become when our paycheck is taken away. We can't get by without money. In the Sermon on the Mount, Jesus made a relevant statement.

> *No one can serve two masters; for either he will hate the one and love the other, or else he will be loyal to the one and despise the other. You cannot serve God and mammon.* (Matt. 6:24)

Jesus said you cannot serve two masters. We have always thought that any effort to become wealthy was somehow serving mammon or money. If we stay poor then we could not be serving money since we have so little of it.

Yet, in spite of this belief, we depend so much on the paycheck at the end of the week that our whole life is scheduled around the need to work for it so that we can pay our bills and have enough to eat. We serve that check. It controls our time, our thoughts, and our actions.

The wealthy have learned to make investments that bring in money without controlling every minute of their schedule. They make the money work for them, which leaves them free to pursue other interests, such as serving God. The average person works to produce something. The wealthy have gone beyond producing and have become multipliers; it was the servants who learned to multiply the minas that were considered "good and faithful."

I am not saying you should just go out and quit your job and start investing in stocks. If you haven't taken the time to become financially literate, you will just make your situation worse. Instead, you need to start learning how investments work and make plans to put yourself in a position to take advantage

> The wealthy make money work for them.

of that knowledge so you can make yourself a good and faithful servant. God wants His kids to start serving His kingdom instead of serving Money.

The Average Person Has a Belief That Was Developed from Childhood

Go to school. Get good grades. Graduate from high school and go to college. Find a good, secure job and work faithfully and diligently at it. If you do these things you will get regular salary raises and promotions, buy a nice house and a nice car and live comfortably until you grow old, when you can no longer afford your house and car and have to move to a smaller house and eventually die with little or nothing to pass on to your children except maybe enough to bury you.

There is nothing wrong with getting good grades and graduating from school and working hard at a good job. Everything we do should be done the best that we can. But all too often, we find that a person spends years working for a corporation, expecting to have a nice comfortable retirement. Then one day the corporation says, "We're losing too much money. Let's downsize." By eliminating some of the higher-paid employees, the company profits improve.

And who are the higher-paid employees? The ones that have been there the longest. So suddenly the secure job is gone and a comparable job in another company is not available because the other corporations have done the same thing. So this person has to take a lesser-paying job just to survive and now runs the very real risk of losing his house, car, and security. Money has demonstrated a considerable control over his life.

While all of that is happening, the profits of the company increased. The company's stock went up and the wealthy who invested in the company made all kinds of money while the average guy worried. The rich get richer and the poor get poorer. It happens because the wealthy don't think about money in the same way as the poor. They have become financially literate enough to make money serve them.

The Average Person Buys Liabilities Instead of Assets

The average person, as he gets raises and accumulates a little bit of money, buys a better house, a bigger car, or nicer clothes. All of these things are expenses. They are things that take money away from us.

The wealthy minimize their liabilities and buy assets—things that increase money, things that create dividends. They buy stocks and bonds and real estate that give them income. They cause their money to multiply rather than just spending it. They plant seed for a harvest while the average person is eating his. The key to becoming wealthy is not to win the lottery. The most important thing is your attitude. When you begin to have the attitude of a millionaire, you will be well on your way to becoming a millionaire. It is absolutely essential that you learn how money works.

There are many good books available that will help you learn what you need to know. Without that knowledge, you will never be able to manage money in a profitable way. Set your attitude to educate yourself in financial matters. Purpose in your heart to become financially literate.

If we can take anything from the thoughts of this chapter, it should be that God is pleased with people who take what He has given them and multiply it. He wants His people to have great wealth because He has called them to do things that require much money. Without money they can't do what He has called them to do. Wrong attitudes toward money become an insurmountable problem to fulfilling God's will. We can choose to ignore money because we think it

> When you begin to have the attitude of a millionaire, you will be well on your way to becoming a millionaire.

is spiritual to do so or we can choose to accumulate wealth just for our own comfort. Either attitude will prevent us from gaining the kind of wealth that God intends. Fear of loss and the desire for things intensified by ignorance steals wealth.

Chapter 2 Summary

Attitude Determines Altitude

What is in the heart will eventually come out. The attitude hidden behind the front will bear fruit and it will limit your potential. You need to adjust your attitude so you begin thinking like a millionaire.

Keys to Right Attitudes

1. You will never achieve or succeed in life higher than your attitude.
2. Attitude has its roots in words and its fruit in actions.
3. What we speak both reflects our attitude and molds it.
4. Your behavior is directly connected to what you believe in your heart. Good attitude produces good action, bad attitude produces bad action.
5. Attitudes are never content until they are expressed.
6. Attitude is your best friend or your worst enemy.
7. Attitude is the library of your past, the speaker of your present, and the prophet of your future.
8. Attitude is a measure of maturity.
9. Bad attitudes might be justified, but they will still hold you back.

Ask yourself, "How important is money?"

People who work hard for a barely adequate paycheck and who get upset if it is a few dollars short are allowing that paycheck to control their lives. Even though such people might say that money doesn't matter, their behavior says otherwise. They devote great amounts of energy and time to their paycheck.

If you took everything that the Word of God teaches us and condensed it down to its simplest form, you would find that: God is interested in the intent of the heart.

It is the love of money that is evil, not money itself.

The Biblical Concept of Wealth
(Taken from Malachi 3)

When a farmer plants a seed, it multiplies. A farmer in biblical times understood what had to be done to insure future harvests.

1. The Tithe: The tithe, or a tenth, was the only thing God required. The tithe guaranteed that God would protect the rest of the harvest from the destroyer.
2. The Offering: Giving an offering, anything over and above the tithe, was planting a spiritual seed. It brought a spiritual blessing. It opened the windows of heaven and caused multiplication of whatever seed was planted.
3. Seed Planted in the Earth: The offering did not bring money. It brought blessing. But there needed to be something to bless. For that, a portion of the seed must be planted in the earth.
4. Only after giving a tithe, an offering, and investing, did the farmer eat what was left.

The same principle holds true with our income today.

1. The tithe protects our possessions.
2. Offerings bring spiritual blessing on the work of our hands.
3. Investments are what can be multiplied by the spiritual blessing.

The Parable of the Minas (Luk. 19:11–27) demonstrates that Jesus expects us to put our resources to work, that is, invest them, not sit on them and remain poor. The only place Jesus uses the words, "good and faithful servant," is in the context of putting money to work.

How the Wealthy Think

The average person works for money. The wealthy make money work for them.

The average person has a goal from childhood to finish school, get a good job with a regular salary, and retire with just enough to get by. The wealthy set a goal of making investments and retiring early so they can devote their time to things other than a job.

The average person buys liabilities, things that take money from him. The wealthy buy assets that bring money to them.

3

Light a Fire

A MAN WAS DRIVING THROUGH THE COUNTRY ONE DAY WHEN HIS CAR broke down. He was in front of a country farmhouse and while someone was working on it, he decided to join an old farmer who was sitting in a rocking chair on the front porch and rocking back and forth, with a straw in his mouth. Just to make conversation the man asked, "Hey, how's the wheat growing?"

The farmer, without any change of expression, said, "I didn't plant any wheat this year. I was afraid there would be a drought."

"Well," asked the man, "then how's the corn growing?"

"Didn't plant any corn either. Afraid there would be too much rain and wash the seed away."

"Well, then, how's the cotton growing?" the man asked.

"I didn't plant any cotton this year. Afraid the boll weevil would come and eat it all up."

The man, somewhat perplexed, finally asked, "What did you plant?"

The farmer leaned back and said, "I didn't plant nothin' this year. I just played it safe."

* * *

It is absolutely essential that we become financially literate before we begin taking the risks inherent in investment. The Word tells us that a fool and his money are soon separated. Money without financial literacy is money soon gone.

But "no investment" is nearly as bad as "foolish investment." We've been playing it safe far too long. We have been dreamers to some extent. We've even been a little lazy. Many of us have learned to confess prosperity Scriptures every day but we don't actually have a passion to do anything more than talk. We have to eventually do something. I cannot overemphasize the importance of learning what you are doing before you do it but without a passion to act on your knowledge, it is useless. Do something, even if all you are doing is reading some books.

> A vision without action is just a hallucination.

A vision without action is just a hallucination. Action without a vision is random activity. It takes a combination of passion and discipline to accomplish anything. Ask yourself, Are you a blaze or a smoldering ash? Consider the words of Matthew 5:14–16:

> *You are the light of the world. A city that is set on a hill cannot be hidden. Nor do they light a lamp and put it under a basket, but on a lampstand, and it gives light to all who are in the house. Let your light so shine before men, that they may see your good works and glorify your Father in heaven.*

The word "light" occurs four times in this passage, but three different Greek words are used. The first is *phos*, in verse 14 and again in verse 16. It refers to the light emitted by a lamp or a fire. It has the connotation of expressing thoughts He has given you concerning your destiny and your future, that we should speak those thoughts out.

The second instance of the word "light," in verse 15, is *kaio*.

It actually means "to set on fire." The third, in verse 16, is *lam-pas*. It refers to a lamp or torch and means "to have the power to make manifest the passion we are set on fire with."[1]

All three verses indicate that being the light of the world is not a passive state of being but rather an action we initiate. You don't become the light of the world by sitting back and glowing. You do it by lighting a fire and speaking out and manifesting God's plans for your life.

Speaking out is easy to understand. We confess the Word as it applies to us. But what is meant by manifesting our destiny? How do we do that? The last phrase in this passage tells us that it is by your "good works." This can mean the way you live your life or the things you do in church or for one another. But the word used here specifically means your production or the things that you produce.

If I might paraphrase the message of this passage, we cause people to glorify the Father when they see how we set on fire, get excited about, and manifest the destiny God has for us in such a way that we produce. Our production directly results in the Father being glorified.

Many passages of Scripture point to the desire of God to see His people living in wealth so that they can represent Him to the rest of the world. Isaiah gives another example: "Arise, shine; for your light has come! And the glory of the Lord is risen upon you" (Isa. 60:1). The word "arise" actually means "to accomplish, perform, and produce fruit, to get a passion for, to let your light shine." Jesus, the light of the world, the Word, is the light that has come, and it is precisely because He has come that the glory of the Lord is risen upon you.

The word "glory" literally means "to have honor, splendor, power, great wealth and authority." It has to do with fame, dignity, and riches. When the glory of the power of God has come upon you it is because He wants you to operate in great fame and wealth. He wants people who will step forward and take on the role of leadership in His kingdom. We are a part of the Abrahamic covenant in which God said, "I will make your name great; and you shall be a blessing. . . . In you all the families of the earth shall be blessed" (Gen. 12:2–3). There is a chapter in Proverbs that speaks of the value of wisdom. Wisdom says, "I love those who love me, and those who seek me diligently will find me" (Prov. 8:17).

We can safely say that the text speaks directly of Jesus, since we know that He is the wisdom, the enlightenment of God because of another verse: "But of Him you are in Christ Jesus, who became for us wisdom from God—and righteousness and sanctification and redemption" (1 Cor. 1:30).

The next verse in Proverbs 8 says, "Riches and honor are with me, enduring riches and righteousness" (8:18). We just read that Jesus is also our righteousness. Proverbs makes Him the source of riches and honor as well. Continuing to the next verse: "My fruit is better than gold, yes, than fine gold, and my revenue than choice silver" (8:19). Many try to point to this verse to say that God is not interested in money, but only in spiritual blessings. But the next verses tell a different story,

> *I traverse the way of righteousness,*
> *In the midst of the paths of justice,*
> *That I may cause those who love me to inherit wealth,*
> *That I may fill their treasuries.*
> *The Lord possessed me at the beginning of His way,*
> *Before His works of old.*
> *I have been established from everlasting,*
> *From the beginning, before there was ever an earth.*
>   (8:20–23)

God said that those who experience His fruit, which is better than gold, will also inherit wealth, and that this was God's plan before the earth existed. Before there even was wealth, God had in mind to fill your treasuries and give you an inheritance of great wealth. It is not stretching the truth to say that God created the wealth of earth precisely because He wanted His people to have it.

I need to keep emphasizing these things because the church has become so accustomed to thinking poverty is spiritual that it affects everything we do. Such thinking robs us of our passion. We say that we believe God wants us to prosper, but deep down we have reservations about it and feel that maybe we are somehow violating holy ground when we speak of material wealth.

> Right attitudes will keep you from going in the wrong direction, but without passion you will not go in any direction at all.

We began this study by talking about the importance of attitudes. Attitude is how you think. Passion is how you feel. It is the product of the attitudes and intentions of the heart. Right attitudes will keep you from going in the wrong direction, but without passion you will not go in any direction at all.

Developing a Passion for Prosperity

Before I was married, Maureen lived up in Duluth. I lived down in Minneapolis-St. Paul. Being a young man I had a certain passion. I didn't mind driving four hours to Duluth after school in order to spend a little time with Maureen . . . and then drive four hours back in time for school in the morning. I had a passion burning in my veins.

I understood from the beginning that I was dating the perfect picture of Judeo-Christian morality, so it became very clear very early that in order to have fulfillment of the passion burning in me, I would have to demonstrate a total commitment—marriage.

But when you truly have a passion for something, you will do anything to fulfill it, even if what you have to do is bring the passion under control and focus it in the right direction. You can see why I started with attitudes rather than passion. Passion can be dangerous if the foundational attitudes are not right.

A literal rendering of the statement of Jesus in Matthew 11:12 is "From the days of John the Baptist until now the kingdom of heaven suffers violence and violent men take it for themselves by force." Jesus is not advocating violence. He is describing the passion that His people must have if they are to inherit the blessings that God has for them in His kingdom. They must forcefully forge ahead without anything distracting them from their purpose. They must have a passion to do whatever it takes to succeed.

Understand that passion can be misdirected. In the parable of the sower, the seed is prevented from multiplying by the "cares of this world and the deceitfulness of riches" (Matt. 13:22). The desire for things is nothing more than greed. You can have a passion for wealth that is entirely based on greed. The comments in the Bible that sound anti-wealth are all directed at greed.

God wants His people to prosper so that they can be generous, not greedy. A passion to gain wealth so that you can give it away is a very godly thing. Your passion should be to leave an inheritance for your children's children. If your passion is rooted in greed, you need to bring it under control and redirect it. One good way to change it is by giving things away. Generosity will cure you quickly.

> God wants His people to prosper so that they can be generous, not greedy.

To summarize what we have said thus far, you have to develop the attitude of the wealthy—you must think like a millionaire and have a passion to gain wealth so that you will actually go and do what you need to do to become wealthy. The most important thing you need to do is become financially literate. If you really have a passion, you will make yourself study.

From a Vision to a Cause

At this point you may be asking, "How can I develop a passion if I don't already have it?" It begins with your attitude, but there is one further point that needs to be made. Passion is directly related to the thoughts and intents of the heart. Put in its simplest form, you will do what you believe. The belief system that you support in your heart will always dictate your behavior. If you want to change your behavior, then you must change your belief system. You must change your attitudes.

You also must have a vision, that is, specific goals toward which you are working. But there is a difference between a vision and a cause. It is critical that you develop not only a vision but that it be connected to a cause.

Martin Luther King Jr. said the immortal words, "I have a dream." He had a vision toward which he directed his life. But in reality, he was speaking of more than a vision. He had a cause. A cause is something that never dies. A vision can change, and frequently does, but a cause continues until it is fulfilled. Martin Luther King Jr.'s cause did not stop when he died. It will continue until it is accomplished. The drive to see equality and harmony between people of all races and backgrounds, to see every person, regardless of where they came from, experience all the promises of God, is a cause bigger than King's personal vision for his life.

People live for a vision, but they will die for a cause. You possess a vision but a cause possesses you. A vision excites but a cause gives you power. What is the cause in your life? It is directly connected to your destiny, to what God created you to do and to be. Connect your vision and your attitudes to a cause and your passion will follow.

A passion to gain wealth will drive you to learn some basic things. There are certain skills that you simply cannot do without. Here are four things that every wealthy person has some grasp of.

First, and probably the most fundamental, you have to become adept at basic accounting. If you can't make sense out of your checking account, then you certainly aren't ready to handle millions of dollars. Many people do not even understand how to balance their checkbook, much less do a balance sheet. I have known many who sit down each month with their bank statement in one hand and their checkbook in the other and, if the final balance in each one does not match, they simply erase the number in the checkbook and replace it with the balance in the statement.

> People live for a vision, but they will die for a cause.

The Bible instructs us to become good stewards of what He has given us. That means that we take the money that comes to us from work and we decide what to do with it. God asks for ten percent, which leaves ninety percent for us to handle. It really is not ours. It all belongs to God anyway, but He asks us to be good stewards of it.

If you get to the middle of the month and don't know where you stand financially, or if you are writing checks that are bouncing, or if you're not paying off your debt effectively, then you are not managing God's money very well. In fact, you are mismanaging it. Don't expect God to bless you with a whole lot more until you learn to handle what you have. It is an unchangeable principle of the kingdom of God that you learn to be faithful in small things before you move on to bigger ones. Learn to balance your checkbook first. Then learn bookkeeping. Then think about buying stocks. If you get these three out of order you will have problems.

The second thing you need to learn is how investments work. Before you risk hard-earned money, you need to know the science, the strategies, and the formulas that good investors know. You are not necessarily ready to become an investor just because you've read three chapters of this book. You still don't know what you are doing. Any investment, whether it be real estate, stocks, bonds, or a business, carries some risk. If you do not consider the risks, then you become a foolish investor—and a fool and his money are soon parted. If you understand how the system works, then your risks are calculated and you will more often make money than lose it.

Third, you need to develop an understanding that the market, whether it be stocks, real estate, investments or bonds, is emotionally driven. If someone who appears to know what they are talking about, such as the Federal Reserve Chairman or an economic expert, says that a recession is expected within the next six months and the media picks up the story and broadcasts it into every home in America, fear grips investors and they begin to prepare themselves for the worst. Before long we actually are going into a recession.

Those who think like millionaires, however, see the opportunity rather than the problem. They actually trick the poor into holding and hoarding their money in order to be ready for the recession. That drives the stock market down. The wealthy buy at the low price and, as soon as they do, the market gains ground, the recession comes to an end and the wealthy have made billions of dollars off of your money that was stuck in a bank for two or three percent interest. At the same time you probably got a credit card from the same bank and ran it up so that you wouldn't feel the effects of the recession, and now you're paying eighteen percent interest to use your money. The market is emotionally driven.

There are seventy million baby boomers in America. They control the finances and the money of the nation. The wealthiest people in the country are baby boomers. They also spend the most. They all want to live in a half-million-dollar home. They want to drive a Lexus. They will buy anything that helps them enjoy life. They spend emotionally.

When you understand that, then you realize that they will be retiring around the year 2010 to 2015 and when they do, they will downsize. They will sell their big houses and cars. Those houses will be cheap because the market will be flooded with them. They will begin to pull their stocks, which will cause the market to falter and come back down. The next ten years will be some of the best America has ever known. If you understand the market you will be in a position to take advantage of that, but you need to study the market and become familiar with every aspect of it.

A fourth thing to learn is the tax laws of America. The rich today do not pay taxes. Those who are professionals, the doctors and lawyers, and those who are employed and working, spend thirty to fifty percent of their income on taxes. That means you are probably working the first four months of the year just for the government. You don't have a penny of your own until about the first of April or May.

In 1923, the government went to the people and asked them to vote to levy the heaviest taxes against corporations and rich people. It was a brilliant idea called income tax. The more money you make the more taxes you pay. That way the poor would not have to support a huge tax burden. The poor were in favor of that idea and, since they accounted for the most votes, it was passed.

The point is that the rich understood taxes better than the poor. They worked the system, lobbied in Congress, inserted loopholes, and learned ways to get around having to pay the taxes. The law was supposed to relieve the poor but, because they did not understand taxes, because they did not have financial literacy, it all backfired in a very short time. The wealthy pay almost no taxes because they are financially literate enough to make the system work for them. To do the same, you do not have to do anything illegal, but you do have to be smart.

Becoming an Investor

These are all things that you need to know. If you really have a passion to gain wealth, then your passion will drive you to learn all that you need to know. It will light a fire in you that won't stop until you have attained your goals. You might be thinking at this point that this sounds like a lot of work. It is. There is no such thing as gaining wealth without some effort. If you are not will-ing to make the effort, then you don't really have a passion. You

> If you really have a passion to gain wealth, then your passion will drive you to learn all that you need to know.

have a desire that will produce a lot of talk but never spur you into action. You will fit into one of four categories in life.

The Employee

The first and most common is the employee. The employee is the person who has a job working for someone else. His income is based entirely on his position. It doesn't matter how good he is or how smart. He fills a position for which he makes a certain amount of money and he is locked into it.

If he works hard and is faithful to his job, his income will prob-ably go up in small amounts. If he is fortunate, those raises will keep pace with inflation. God can bless the employee who tithes and gives offerings. He can get raises and promotions, advancements and benefits. But the employee works for money. Any blessings that

God gives him in his job have to be channeled through the will of another person, the Employer. There is only so much that can happen within that framework. The employee buys liabilities. He typically pays about thirty percent of his income into taxes. When he is old he will retire with maybe enough money to bury himself. He will leave no posterity for his children.

The Self-Employed

The second category is the self-employed, who owns a job. He might be a dentist, a lawyer, a doctor, real estate agent, hair stylist, or salesperson, but he works for himself. He makes money and buys a few assets, but for the most part he works for money. Doctors and lawyers only make about $87,000 per year. To most employees that seems like a lot of money, but compared to the millions the wealthy make, it is not much at all. The self-employed buys a nice house, nice car, and looks wealthy. But he is still buying liabilities and he still is locked into office hours every day. He is still paying fifty percent of his income in taxes. His position is not really much different than the employee's—he just has better credit.

The Business Owner

The third category is the business owner. A business owner is similar to someone who is self-employed. A small mom-and-pop operation has the same restrictions as that of someone who is self-employed, but as a business owner expands his business and causes it to grow, he creates a system that makes money for him. A business has unlimited potential for growth. A business owner is limited only by his own vision. He finds himself in a position of transition between working for money and making money work for him. He usually works very hard to manage the business, and the bigger it gets, the more others do the work. He is really getting other people to make money for him. He is still likely to buy liabilities, but he is building assets at the same time. These assets will put money in his pocket instead of taking it out.

The Investor

The fourth category is the investor. He may have started as an employee or self-employed, and he may even have grown to the level of business owner. The difference is that he learned some things along the way about how money works. He developed a passion for gaining wealth, and it caused him to do a few things the employee and self-employed usually don't do. He found a way to set a little money aside so that he could invest it. He studied to learn how investments work, that is, he became financially literate. Then he actually took his investment money and invested it. As a result, his investments began to bring in money with virtually no effort on his part. He learned to make money work for him.

The life of the investor is a life that is attainable for anyone who has enough passion to make some changes in how he lives. It is not really that complicated. If you are an employee, you have to discipline yourself to set aside some money for investment. If you are like most people you spend every penny as soon as you have it, trying to buy things that will make your life comfortable or make you look wealthier than you really are. The first step is to stop trying to live like the

> The life of the investor is a life that is attainable for anyone who has enough passion to make some changes in how he lives.

Vanderbilts on the Smith's wages. You will then have a few dollars left over at the end of the month that you can use to build your future.

Where to Invest

What should you invest in? The first thing should be in God. Get into the habit of taking your tithes and offerings off the top of your paycheck. Next, pay yourself. Last, pay expenses. If there is not enough money to do all three, then leave yourself out and pay God first, then expenses. Stop buying liabilities so you can bring your expenses down to the point that you can pay yourself and still cover your expenses. Everyone can set aside some money. For most of us, it's a matter of cutting out a soda or bag of chips during the day. The money will add up pretty quickly. When your expenses are low enough, you can start giving yourself ten percent in addition to the ten percent you are already giving God. Invest ten percent of your income and in five years you will be amazed how much your financial situation has changed.

This principle is prevalent throughout the Bible if we will only take notice of it. We mentioned Joseph when we talked about how much attitude matters. If we look at what he did after he rose to be second in charge of Egypt, we will find that he was using sound investment practices. The story begins in Genesis 41. Joseph had been sold into slavery by his brothers, worked for Potiphar until he was wrongly accused of attempted rape by Potiphar's wife, stuck in prison for a time and eventually elevated to a position second only to Pharaoh, because of his ability to interpret a dream that Pharaoh had. According to the dream there would be seven plentiful years followed by seven years of famine. Joseph took on the responsibility of managing Egypt's resources in preparation for the lean years.

Joseph was thirty years old when he stood before Pharaoh king of Egypt. And Joseph went out from the presence of Pharaoh, and went throughout all the land of Egypt. Now in the seven plentiful years the ground brought forth abundantly. So he gathered up all

*the food of the seven years which were in the land of Egypt, and
laid up the food in the cities; he laid up in every city the food of the
fields which surrounded them. Joseph gathered very much grain,
as the sand of the sea, until he stopped counting, for it was without number.* (Gen. 41:46–49)

Joseph was investing in commodities. He was cornering the
market in such a way that he would be the only one who had any
commodities when the time of famine came. He was investing.
The wisdom of his operation became apparent when the good
years were over.

*Then the seven years of plenty which were in the land of Egypt
ended, and the seven years of famine began to come, as Joseph had
said. The famine was in all lands, but in all the land of Egypt there
was bread. So when all the land of Egypt was famished, the people
cried to Pharaoh for bread. Then Pharaoh said to all the Egyptians,
"Go to Joseph; whatever he says to you, do." The famine was over
all the face of the earth, and Joseph opened all the storehouses and
sold to the Egyptians. And the famine became severe in the land
of Egypt. So all countries came to Joseph in Egypt to buy grain,
because the famine was severe in all lands.* (Gen. 41:53–57)

While we are focusing on the business aspects of what Joseph did in Egypt, it is no small thing that he was the only one
in all of Egypt who seemed to know what was going on. Even
Pharaoh didn't know what to do. He just sent people to Joseph.
"Whatever he says to you, do." It is a measure of how much
God's hand was on Joseph that he could go from prison to such
a position of respect in such a short time.

Joseph actually brought in profit from his investments. It
is worth noticing that he also proved to be the salvation of the
whole world, since no one else had been organized enough or

foresighted enough to be ready for the opportunity. They came to him to buy, buy, and buy some more. Joseph made a lot of money.

> *And Joseph gathered up all the money that was found in the land of Egypt and in the land of Canaan, for the grain which they bought; and Joseph brought the money into Pharaoh's house. So when the money failed in the land of Egypt and in the land of Canaan, all the Egyptians came to Joseph and said, "Give us bread, for why should we die in your presence? For the money has failed." (Gen. 47:14–15)*

Money failed in the land because Joseph had all of it. He became so prosperous that he not only made a lot of money, he made all the money! No one else had any. But that was not the end of it.

> *Then Joseph said, "Give your livestock, and I will give you bread for your livestock, if the money is gone." So they brought their livestock to Joseph, and Joseph gave them bread in exchange for the horses, the flocks, the cattle of the herds, and for the donkeys. Thus he fed them with bread in exchange for all their livestock that year. (Gen. 47:16–17)*

By the end of that year Joseph not only had all of the money in the land but also all of the livestock. But he still wasn't finished.

> *When that year had ended, they came to him the next year and said to him, "We will not hide from my lord that our money is gone; my lord also has our herds of livestock. There is nothing left in the sight of my lord but our bodies and our lands. Why should we die before your eyes, both we and our land? Buy us and our land for bread, and we and our land will be servants of Pharaoh; give us seed, that we may live and not die, that the land may not be desolate." Then*

*Joseph bought all the land of Egypt for Pharaoh; for every man of
the Egyptians sold his field, because the famine was severe upon
them. So the land became Pharaoh's.* (Gen. 47:18–20)

Joseph cornered all the money and all the livestock and also
became a real estate czar. But then he took it even a step further:

*Then Joseph said to the people, "Indeed I have bought you and
your land this day for Pharaoh. Look, here is seed for you, and you
shall sow the land. And it shall come to pass in the harvest that
you shall give one-fifth to Pharaoh. Four-fifths shall be your own,
as seed for the field and for your food, for those of your households
and as food for your little ones."* (Gen. 47:23–24)

Once Joseph owned everything in the country he loaned it all
back to the people he had gotten it from and charged them twenty
percent for the use of their own produce. And not only that, but
he was wise enough and blessed enough when it was over that no
one thought they were being cheated. In fact they thanked him:
"So they said, 'You have saved our lives; let us find favor in the
sight of my lord'" (Gen. 47:25).

There are several lessons here. The first thing we should see is
how money is made. Joseph made intelligent investments based
on his knowledge of the market. As a result, he acquired everything in the land. Second, he was the only one who did it. No one
else made money because no one else made the same kinds of
investments. He was the only one with the foresight to prepare
and the wisdom to invest in the right things.

You might say Joseph was only making money for Pharaoh.
Yet while Pharaoh actually had the money, it should be noted that
Joseph was a primary beneficiary of this wealth. He was also in
a position to rescue his family, God's chosen people. The difficult
times were not difficult for them. They were a golden opportunity.
The money went to Pharaoh for the time being, but Moses took

it when he led Israel out of Egypt . . . ultimately it financed God's people.

Joseph demonstrated what passion should be. His passion was not simply to get rich. It was to serve God. But serving God meant having an attitude that took advantage of every opportunity to multiply everything under his hand. It also meant acting with loyalty, integrity, and diligence. As a result, God blessed everything he touched to such an extent that he influenced the course of the entire world.

Chapter 3 Summary

Light a Fire

You must develop a passion so you will actually move forward. Attitude is how you think. Passion is how you feel. Become financially literate so you won't make foolish investments. But you must then have a passion to act on that knowledge.

Keys to Developing Passion

1. Vision with action will produce. A vision without action is just a hallucination.
2. It takes a combination of passion and discipline to succeed.
3. Passion changes *have to* into *want to* and you start to enjoy the climb as much as reaching the top.

Our passion should come from our calling. We are called to be the light of the world (Matt. 5:14–16). This involves three aspects of light:

1. *Phos*: Expressing the thoughts God has given you about your destiny.
2. *Kaio*: To set on fire.
3. *Lampas*: To have the power to make manifest the passion we are set on fire with.[2]

You become the light of the world by lighting a fire of passion, speaking out, and manifesting God's plans for your life.

You manifest your destiny by your "good works," that is, by the things you produce.

We cause people to glorify the Father when they see how we set on fire, get excited about, and manifest the destiny God has for us in such a way that we produce.

Get a Passion

1. Right attitudes will keep you from going in the wrong direction, but without passion you will go in no direction at all.
2. If you have a passion for something, you will do whatever it takes to fulfill it.
3. Passion is directly related to the thoughts and intents of the heart.

Get a Cause

It is important to not only develop a vision but also connect it to a cause.

1. A vision can change but a cause continues until it is fulfilled.
2. People will live for a vision, but they will die for a cause.
3. You possess a vision, but a cause possesses you.
4. A vision excites, but a cause gives power.

Connect your vision and your attitudes to a cause and your passion will follow.

Essential Skills of the Wealthy Person

1. Become adept at accounting.
2. Learn how investments work.
3. Understand that the marketplace is emotionally driven. Look for opportunities rather than reacting to circumstances.
4. Learn the tax laws of America and how to take advantage of every legal loophole.

4

Get over It

WHEN I WAS ABOUT EIGHT YEARS OLD I BOUGHT A COMIC BOOK ABOUT Scrooge McDuck. I still love Uncle Scrooge. I loved all the stories about him, but this particular issue remains vividly in my mind even today. Uncle Scrooge was fabulously wealthy. In one of the opening frames, he was pictured sitting in the middle of his billions of dollars, bathing in it, throwing money in the air. Yet then he experienced a series of setbacks and financial disasters that resulted in his losing everything. He was eventually homeless, his clothes in tatters, a hole in his hat. Destitute, he wandered along the street, penniless.

As he was walking, he noticed a nickel. He reached down and picked it up. Continuing along, he saw some kids fishing. They had caught a number of fish, so he offered them the nickel in exchange for the fish. He continued down the street to a restaurant where he sold the fish for several dollars. He used the dollars to buy a scooter. Then he saw someone whose car had broken down. The story continued with one trade after another until Scrooge McDuck had all his money back.

There is a principle here we need to learn. It just makes good sense to copy the behavior of the successful. If you want to be thin, do what thin people do. If you want to be smart, do what smart people do. If you want to be fat, do what fat people do. If you want to be wealthy, do what wealthy people do.

Uncle Scrooge experienced failure but it did not shake his confidence in the process of making money. He knew he would make it back. So he looked for an opportunity to begin investing in something. Most people in the same position would just give up and hope they could find enough charity to enable them to survive. The wealthy have a whole different approach to setbacks, for they are not afraid of failure. These are characteristics of the wealthy that we can and should emulate.

The Wealthy Make No Small Plans

We know that the Word says not to despise small beginnings. Things that start small can grow. But too often we are so pleased with the initial small successes that we don't press on to the bigger victories. We become like the man who started his day by making a list of things he needed to do. The list included big things and small things, from calling his mom to painting the house. As soon as he finished writing the list, he sat down and phoned his mom. Checking that item off the list, he felt so good about the list and his accomplishment that he sat down to have a cup of coffee and watch television to celebrate. Of course nothing else on the list got done. A poor person will make something he can sell and then feel satisfied after selling just a few hundred. A millionaire will find a way to get others to make it and sell it for him and will sell a few million.

The Wealthy Do What They Fear

You can recognize a successful person because he does not shy away from things he is afraid of. Instead, he challenges those things. The thrill of overcoming makes the effort worthwhile. Public speaking is a good example of a fear that many have. If you run and hide every time you are called upon to address a group of people, then you are running from your fears. The wealthy do whatever they have to in order to become adept at it.

The Wealthy Prepare Themselves

They anticipate the direction they are going and do everything they can to be ready for it. Much of what we have already discussed in the first three chapters is about preparation. Learning how to do bookkeeping, how investments work, what the market is like, and how the tax laws operate are areas of financial literacy that you need to know to prepare yourself.

> You can recognize a successful person because he does not shy away from things he is afraid of.

The wealthy weren't born with this knowledge; they learned it. They prepared. The time to learn how to do anything is before you have to do it, not afterward. The time to learn about marriage is before you are married. The time to learn how to handle money is before you have it. If you don't learn it before, then you won't have the money very long. Become financially literate and you will minimize your chances of failure. Read and study.

The Wealthy Have Heart

They don't let the circumstances ever get them down. Just like Uncle Scrooge, if they lose everything, they just start looking for ways to get it back. They are confident and optimistic.

The Wealthy Risk Failure

A simple fact that is often overlooked is that you cannot win if you do not play. If you never take any risks, then you will never fail, but you will also never succeed. Failure does not mean the end. It should mean a lesson that will better prepare you for the next effort. All successful investors have some failures in their lives. But they move on and try not to make the same mistakes again. With every new project the chance of failure becomes less. Failure is not the enemy of success, but rather the teacher of success. Edison tried the light bulb 3,960 times before he succeeded. He could have given up at any point but with each failure he eliminated one more thing that didn't work. Eventually he found the right one.

In all five of these characteristics of the wealthy, I am really talking about faith. The wealthy have an absolute confidence that they will succeed. Even if they fail, it is only a learning step to success and not the last word. They think big. They challenge their fears. They prepare for success. They have heart and are not afraid of failure. Such confidence is the result of a settled conviction, a belief in success. That is faith. Even those investors who are not believers have this faith. In their case it is faith in their own abilities. How much more should believers have confidence in success when they have the creator of the universe backing them? So you've failed in the past or you've just failed to try. Get over it. You need to get faith instead.

> The wealthy have an absolute confidence that they will succeed.

The Role of Miracles

I have not spoken much up to this point about miracles because we must first learn the principles of the Word and not rely constantly on miracles. Miracles will not make you wealthy. Biblical principles will. But that does not mean I don't believe in miracles. God is a miracle-working God. He sometimes has to bail us out of circumstances that we have gotten ourselves into. It is better to learn the principles from the Word of God and live by them than to need a financial miracle, but He is there for those days that we are too thick-headed or slow in grasping the truth. We occasionally have to operate in grace. That is good to know because it means that God will miraculously prevent your failures from dooming you to poverty for the rest of your life. He will bring you through them. Your job is to prepare in every way that you know how and then do something. God will cover you when your heart is right.

Many years ago Maureen and I sat down to write checks. We wrote one to Harry Greenwood, put it in an envelope, and put a stamp on it. The money was not in the bank yet so we intended to wait and mail it when we knew that it was good. I do not believe you should try to send money you don't have and then hope that it will somehow appear in your account before the check clears. That is presumption, not faith. We made a faith commitment but we hadn't mailed the check yet. Our hearts were right.

Then an incident occurred. Somehow the check was accidentally mailed anyway. Well, God had to do something miraculous. I had gold credit. I didn't want a check to bounce and damage my reputation. Yet I'm a tither. I had consistently been giving tithes and offerings. God had to do something.

The same day that the check was mailed, we received a check from the state of Wisconsin. It was a tax refund from seven years earlier. We didn't even know we had a refund coming. God stepped in and used His miraculous provision to cover our mistake. God does do miracles, and that is part of living in faith, but we still need to learn the principles so that we don't need the miracles. But you can have confidence that if you do make mistakes God will not let them destroy you. Failure for God's people is not really failure. It is an opportunity to learn and to build faith.

Overcoming Failure

There are many reasons why people fail. Some of them, we have already addressed. Not having a purpose or a cause is a significant one. Without goals, people have no direction. Neither do they have the drive to do anything. They either flounder or move in circles and they accomplish virtually nothing.

A different problem, but with the same result, is procrastination. You may be one of those people who never does something right now. It is always tomorrow. You talk about wealth. You talk about investments. You talk about real estate. You talk about business. But you are too busy talking to ever actually invest. It's not much good being a goal setter if you are not also a goal getter.

Procrastination is one of the results of a third problem—the lack of self-discipline. It shows up in many places. People who can never get to work on time or meet any kind of a deadline are usually lacking in self-discipline. They have trouble succeeding in business because no one can ever afford to work with them. They are too unreliable to be trusted with any job that matters.

Indiscriminate spending is a fiscal form of no self-discipline. If most people are given a large amount of money, they talk very loudly about investing but they will probably spend it all on things they don't actually need. They justify it, going out to dinner, buying new clothes, maybe buying a new television, all things that they think they have to have. The family has had to watch the old television for a long time now, after all. They will buy liabilities instead of assets and suddenly there is nothing left to invest. Self-discipline will keep you from wasting your resources and having nothing to show for it.

Another factor that keeps people from succeeding is that they are just plain dumb. They make decisions that create financial problems for themselves. They make commitments they can't possibly keep.

A story is told of a man who, upon his retirement, was turning his business over to his son. He gave a few words of advice on his last day. "Son, what made this business successful is reliability and wisdom."

His son asked him, "What do you mean by reliability?"

The man answered, "That means that if you say you will get a job done by Monday morning, then you get it done by Monday morning, even if you have to work the entire weekend and stay up all night on Sunday to get it done."

"Where does wisdom fit in?" asked the son.

"Wisdom is knowing better than to promise it by Monday morning in the first place."

Many fail because they have not developed an attitude of excellence. Everything they do is half-hearted and mediocre. They are average and therefore never stand out from the rest of the crowd. To be successful, you should consistently do ten percent more than anyone else. So few people actually do anything above average that you can be successful on the basis of that one factor alone.

> To be successful, you should consistently do ten percent more than anyone else.

Some lack focus. They try to do too many things and they are unable to do any of them well. Success may mean cutting out activities and projects that do not really connect to your goals.

A related problem is the person who sees himself as a lone ranger. If you are such a person, you probably feel pretty good about yourself because you are the only one with the talent to do it all. No one else is skilled enough and you are indispensable. Unfortunately everyone is expendable. Depending entirely on your own talent to get everything done means that the business will never get any bigger than you. It also means that you will have a tough time investing because you can't trust anyone else. Delegation is a requirement for success.

Pride might be included in the same category. It is not exactly the same but the effect is that you look down on everyone around you and you are never able to incorporate their talents in your projects as a result. The effects are the same as being a lone ranger.

Dishonesty is another character trait that will destroy the trust of people around you. It certainly does not open the doors to God's blessing. It is difficult for Him to bless something not in keeping with His character. Dishonesty will eventually catch up with you. By dishonesty I am not just talking about felony embezzlement. When you take a pen that belongs to your employer, you are practicing dishonesty. When you take a nap or chat idly on the phone with a friend while you are being paid to work, you are stealing time. Dishonesty is a character trait more than an action. And it will bring failure to your endeavors.

Many fail because of their intolerance of others. Any kind of business or investment that will make millions of dollars requires working with other people. If you cannot learn to accept them as they are, you will have trouble. Religious people often have the most trouble tolerating others. They are afraid that being around all that sin will corrupt them, so they sabotage potentially profitable working relationships as a result, to say nothing of the potential for sharing the Gospel message with them.

Fear is another cause of failure. We have already talked about it. The fear of failure will cause a person never to take risks and, while they may avoid failing, it is an absolute certainty that they won't succeed.

Many people use sickness or tiredness as an excuse for failure. They feel a little tired or a little sick and they sit and relax rather than do the things they need to do to succeed. We could devote an entire book just to sickness. Too many people talk themselves into being sick and justify their lack of effort through it. The end result is the same as that of fear. They never do anything that will help them out of the position they are in. Aside from the fact that living by faith means that you learn to walk in health, many of the most successful people in history achieved remarkable things under the most severe handicaps. Their determination and passion empowered them to overcome

> No handicap is really an acceptable excuse if you have the determination to overcome it.

every obstacle. Beethoven wrote and directed his most memorable symphony after he had gone completely deaf. No handicap is really an acceptable excuse if you have the determination to overcome it.

A last cause of failure is also a very common one in the business world. It is the desire to get something for nothing. You will not gain the kind of wealth God wants for you by playing the lottery. There is always some effort involved.

These are some of the primary causes of failure. The point in reviewing them is that failure does not have to be the end of the story. Each failure should teach you a little more about how to do better the next time. Wisdom grows out of experience.

Gaining Wisdom

Wisdom is an invaluable commodity. It will make you successful if you have it.

Happy is the man who finds wisdom,
And the man who gains understanding.
For her proceeds are better than the profits of silver,
And her gain than fine gold.
She is more precious than rubies,
And all the things you may desire cannot compare with her.
Length of days is in her right hand,
In her left hand riches and honor.

Her ways are ways of pleasantness,
And all her paths are peace.
She is a tree of life to those who take hold of her,
And happy are all who retain her. (Prov. 3:13–18)

So possessing wisdom will give you long life, riches, and honor. If you never educate yourself in any other area of finance, you could still improve your position by reading Proverbs every day, just to gain wisdom.

We should ask the question, however, what is wisdom? We usually give it a nice spiritual definition, as though the ability to quote Bible verses makes us wise. But we can look at the life of the wisest man in the Bible, Solomon, and see what it was that was counted as wisdom in him.

The story of Solomon is familiar to most people; it is in 1 Kings 3. Solomon's wealth was renowned throughout the world. This passage of Scripture tells us how he got it. God appeared to Solomon in a dream and told him to ask for any one thing that he wanted. He responded by recounting how God had blessed his father David. Then he asked for the thing he considered absolutely essential.

And Your servant is in the midst of Your people whom You have
chosen, a great people, too numerous to be numbered or counted.
Therefore give to Your servant an understanding heart to judge
Your people, that I may discern between good and evil. For who is
able to judge this great people of Yours? (1 Kgs. 3:8–9)

God was pleased with this response. Solomon asked for wisdom, the one thing that would make everything else possible.

Then God said to him: "Because you have asked this thing, and
have not asked long life for yourself, nor have asked riches for
yourself, nor have asked the life of your enemies, but have asked

for yourself understanding to discern justice, behold, I have done according to your words; see, I have given you a wise and understanding heart, so that there has not been anyone like you before you, nor shall any like you arise after you. And I have also given you what you have not asked: both riches and honor, so that there shall not be anyone like you among the kings all your days."
(1 Kgs. 3:11–13)

So Solomon gained wisdom, but with wisdom came riches and honor. He became the wealthiest man in the world. He also became so famous that people came to see him from all over the world: "And men of all nations, from all the kings of the earth who had heard of his wisdom, came to hear the wisdom of Solomon" (1 Kgs. 4:34).

The Word tells us some details about his wisdom. It involved the spiritual qualities we would normally associate with wisdom—proverbs and songs—but it encompassed some downright earthy things as well.

He spoke three thousand proverbs, and his songs were one thousand and five. Also he spoke of trees, from the cedar tree of Lebanon even to the hyssop that springs out of the wall; he spoke also of animals, of birds, of creeping things, and of fish.
(1 Kgs. 4:32–33)

This wisdom that brings happiness, long life, riches, and honor is more than just a Bible knowledge of spiritual things. It includes an understanding of a vast array of very worldly things. Solomon became wealthy and famous because he learned how the world works. As a result, he made smart investments, intelligent plans, and wise choices in life.

> Solomon became wealthy and famous because he learned how the world works.

And the whole world came to Solomon for his wisdom. That is how it ought to be now. The world should be coming to the people of God to learn how the world works. It should be in the church that we find the best marriage and family relationship classes, the best teaching on health and nutrition, and even the most helpful financial seminars. It is a shame we have shunned so much of this wisdom, and all because we considered it too worldly and not very spiritual.

Notice, too, that Solomon sought wisdom. It was not something he viewed as just nice to have, but he desired it out of his own need. He was in a position where he was overwhelmed by the responsibility placed on him. He felt utterly inadequate for the task of being king. He didn't feel that he could match up to his father David. He didn't feel smart enough or strong enough. The Bible makes it clear Solomon had enemies who wanted him dead. Certainly he was aware of the very real potential for failure.

Most people feel inadequate at some time in their lives, if not for their entire lives. What made Solomon different from them was his desire to learn wisdom. He asked God for it but to achieve it, he still had to read and study and learn. If you have failed or if you feel overwhelmed by everything that is against you and there is no way you will ever achieve great wealth, then I suggest you follow in Solomon's footsteps. Ask God to give you wisdom. Then begin reading, studying, and learning, and not just the Bible, but everything you can find about how the world works, how money works, and how investments work. Solomon didn't just sit down one day and start writing Proverbs. Many of the things in that book can be traced to older books of wisdom in other cultures, especially in Egypt. Solomon studied them and compiled them, adding his own insights as he went. Such study is an integral part of becoming

> When you achieve wisdom, the world will seek you out to ask your advice.

wise. When you achieve wisdom, the world will seek you out to ask your advice.

We began this chapter with the story of Scrooge McDuck. When he lost everything he owned, he reacted by looking for ways to make it all back. He could do that because he understood how money works.

Some of you are saying, "That's fine for a comic book character, but this is real life. What has a duck got to do with me?"

When Maureen and I moved to Arizona, I was out of the ministry for a short time. I ended up working in construction. God prospered me in that job. I went from $7.50 to $27.00 per hour. It was a good job. But then I got laid off. The good job with its good income was gone. I was working for money, living week to week. The money soon ceased. We had no savings account and a total of $450 in a credit reserve. That was it.

I drove home and Maureen and I prayed together. Many would do the same and, because God said to take no thought, they would sit back and wait for money to fall from the sky. Wealth, however, is a fruit of wisdom, and wisdom says you should do something.

One day I went to the store. On the way back I saw an old car sitting in the front yard of a house. God told me to buy it. The owner wanted $500 for it. So I scraped together enough cash to buy it. I had to push it home, but it was a car I could fix. Within a week I sold it for $1,600.

My bills at that time were $800 a month, so in one week I had enough money to live for two months. I made more money doing this than I did working! Maureen and I would go to auctions and pray over cars. We bought about three a week. In a short time we were making three to four thousand dollars every week. Sometimes we just gave cars away because we were so blessed.

The cars we bought were not liabilities. They were assets. They could be turned into a profit very quickly. This is the secret of wealth. In all the books I have read, I have not found anything that is any more complicated than this: Do not buy liabilities.

Buy assets that can be fixed up and resold for more than you paid for them.

Anyone can do this. If you only have twenty dollars, go to some yard sales. Choose the nicer neighborhoods and look for something that needs painting or sewing or some kind of fixing that you can do. On the next Saturday, have a yard sale of your own and sell it for two hundred dollars. Real estate works the same way. Buy property that can be increased in value and sell it for more than you paid for it. Stocks work the same way. Buy low and sell high.

The secret of wealth is not complicated. But it does require that you become financially literate. It does not require that you have a lot to get started—anyone can do it. Opportunities are always there if you learn the system and start looking. You don't have to be a genius. We all have the same sized brain, so the question is how much of it will you use? If you can read, then you can learn. Will you read just enough to pay your bills or will you read to gain wisdom greater than the world has? Will you wallow in failure or get over it and get faith instead?

Chapter 4 Summary

Get over It

If you want to be wealthy, do what the wealthy do.

1. The wealthy make no small plans. A poor person will make something he can sell and then feel satisfied after selling a few hundred. A wealthy person will find a way to get others to make it and sell it for him, and will sell a few million.
2. The wealthy do what they fear. They challenge the things they are afraid of and overcome them.
3. The wealthy prepare themselves. They earn as much as they can to be ready for opportunities.
4. The wealthy are teachable.
5. The wealthy have heart. They don't let circumstances get them down.
6. The wealthy risk failure. They realize that failure is not the enemy of success. It is the teacher of success. Early loss takes off the pressure of attempting to maintain an undefeated season.

The Place of Miracles

God does do miracles to bail us out when we run into a crisis, but He wants us to learn the principles of the Word of God and live in them so that we don't need a miracle.

Thirteen Reasons People Fail

1. They don't have a purpose or a cause.
2. They procrastinate. They talk about wealth but always put off doing something to acquire it until tomorrow.
3. They lack self-discipline. They are unreliable, so no one will work with them, or they spend indiscriminately and don't put anything aside to invest.
4. They make dumb decisions that create problems for themselves or they make commitments they can't keep.
5. They have not developed an attitude of excellence. Consequently, they are average and never stand out from the crowd.
6. They lack focus. They try to do too many things and are unable to do any of them well.
7. They never learn to delegate or to trust others to do the work.
8. They have pride in their own abilities and never incorporate the talents of others.
9. They are dishonest. Others learn not to trust them.
10. They are intolerant and can't work with others.
11. They fear failure, so they never take risks.
12. They use sickness or tiredness as an excuse for doing nothing.
13. They want something for nothing. Success always requires effort.

To overcome these causes of failure, we must seek wisdom, which is a knowledge of how the world works and an understanding of how to use that knowledge for benefit.

5

You Talk Too Much

In the first four chapters, I have tried to change how you think about wealth. I have described several practical aspects of how money works, and I will discuss more through the rest of the book, but it is critical that you develop the right mind-set before you do anything else. If you don't, then wealth will be very difficult to get and to keep.

Up to this point, I have mainly tried to inspire you to:

1. Determine where you are at so you can get your life under control and change your direction.
2. Adjust your attitudes so you begin thinking like a millionaire.
3. Develop a passion so you will actually move forward.
4. Quit making excuses.

All of these depend on developing financial literacy. The trouble is that these are all steps you have to take yourself. No one is going to do the preparation or the work for you. You alone have to make the effort.

You've heard the saying, "You can lead a horse to water but

you can't make him drink." When I was young I had an old workhorse. He was so big it took a ladder to climb up on his back. I was pretty little at the time so he probably seemed bigger than he actually was, but he was still big enough. I grew up in logging country. My father was a logger, so at a very early age I was given responsibility to skid pulp to the road to be hauled to the railroad and then shipped to papermills. My horse was a logging horse trained to skid pulp. I used to skid pulp with him all day and about noon I would lead him down to the creek and try to get him to drink.

If he didn't want to drink, however, there was nothing I could do. I would pull his reins right down close to the water and try to stick his nose in it. But he'd just get mad and lift me right off the ground and throw me out in the brush. You can lead a horse to water but you can't make him drink. I can lead you to the principles of prosperity but I can't make you learn them or live them.

One thing about a horse, though, is that even though you can't make him drink, you can put salt in his oats. In the same way, by showing you examples of people in the Bible who overcame every imaginable adversity and gained great wealth, I hope I am salting your food to make you thirsty enough to drink. By sharing my own experiences, I trust you will become inspired to make important changes. God wants you to have the best. The problem isn't with Him and it's not with the money—the problem is with you.

Preparation for Success

You must prepare yourself to succeed. That's what this book is all about. Charles Kittering said, "I expect to spend the rest of my life in the future, so I want to be reasonably sure what kind of a future it's going to be, and that's my reason for preparing." We went to school and learned to read and write. We learned to do math and studied science and learned some history.

Yet there were three things we did not learn from school:

- how to have a successful marriage
- how to raise children successfully
- how to become wealthy

There are many roads we can take to change all of these situations, but they all lead back to the very simple concept that you must think differently in order to act differently, choose differently, and succeed differently than you have in the past.

Paul spoke about the transformation that must take place in us to escape the world system.

I beseech you therefore, brethren, by the mercies of God, that you present your bodies a living sacrifice, holy, acceptable to God, which is your reasonable service. And do not be conformed to this world, but be transformed by the renewing of your mind, that you may prove what is that good and acceptable and perfect will of God. (Rom. 12:1–2)

What God wants from you is simple—everything you have! He seems to think the complete offering of your body to Him is nothing more than what is reasonable. It is important for us to recognize, however, that the sacrifice God expects of you is a living sacrifice. He does not want to kill you. Dead people don't bring much glory to God. Neither do poor people or sick people. God wants a sacrifice from you that makes your body, your physical, material being, a testimony to His love and power and blessing. That is why He wants you, and that is why He wants you to prosper. What is good for Him is also good for you. God says, "Reasonably, I want body, soul, and spirit because I've got plans for you that are way beyond your plans. They're above your plans."

The second thing to notice is that the sacrifice should be holy and acceptable to God. It is important that you have a right heart, without greed. A desire to be wealthy does not necessarily proceed from greed. There are good reasons to desire wealth and you need to make sure your attitude is right so your sacrifice to God is acceptable and holy. It's not about how much you can get. It's about how much you can give. Can God make you rich for the sake of His kingdom, or will you take the wealth He gives you and squander it on your own appetites, thereby becoming a disgrace to the kingdom of God?

> A desire to be wealthy does not necessarily proceed from greed.

The next thing Paul mentions is how we must not be conformed to the world but instead be transformed. And the method of transformation is through the renewing of your mind. You have to think differently. The biggest area of change in your thinking needs to be in your understanding of what it means to be conformed to this world. We have divided the world into the compartments of "physical" and "spiritual" and assumed everything physical is the world that we were not supposed to be conformed to. But we have to get over that kind of thinking, because God made the physical world just as much as He made the spiritual world. When He told us not to be conformed to the world, He was talking about the system of belief that has resulted from sin. It is the kind of thinking that promotes our comfort over God's purposes.

Jesus said we can know people by their fruit (Matt. 7:16). You can identify the world system in the same way. We are familiar with the fruits of the Spirit—"But the fruit of the Spirit is love, joy, peace, longsuffering, kindness, goodness, faithfulness, gentleness, self-control" (Gal. 5:22–23). The works of the flesh are just as much an indicator of the world system as the fruit of the Spirit is of God's system. Notice that most of these are not actions that people do but manifestations of attitudes or beliefs: "Now the works of the flesh are evident, which are: adultery, fornication, uncleanness, lewdness, idolatry, sorcery, hatred, contentions, jealousies, outbursts of wrath, selfish ambitions, dissensions, heresies, envy, murders, drunkenness, revelries, and the like" (Gal. 5:19–21).

Avoiding wealth is not the same thing as conforming to the world. Quite the contrary. A poverty mentality is more conformed to the world system of belief than gaining wealth with a right heart. The poverty mentality of the world says that you must work hard your whole life, live in poverty, struggle to get by, work for money, pay your bills, buy liabilities, and retire with just enough Social Security to survive. That is the world you are not to conform to. God wants you to be prosperous. He does not want you to adopt the world's way of thinking.

> A poverty mentality is more conformed to the world system of belief than gaining wealth with a right heart.

We have some twisted ideas of what "spiritual" actually means or is. A woman might complain that her husband isn't spiritual, yet he loves her. He loves his kids. He works hard. At the same time you can find a preacher, a mighty man of ministry who is praying for people and seeing great miracles happen everywhere he goes. But his kids hate him. His wife goes to another church. And yet we call him spiritual. Those who put ministry first and family second have not understood God's way of doing things. They are running from the responsibility of taking care of those things that are part of the world they live in. The image is justified by creating a spiritual image of ministry, but the fruit is not there. And we have all heard the phrase "too spiritually minded to be any earthly good."

Jesus didn't walk around all the time in a perpetual spiritual trance. He laughed. He cried. He talked with people. He interacted constantly with the world around Him. He was the ultimate people person. But He never let that get in the way of His primary responsibilities. He constantly concerned Himself with His disciples and never lost sight of His responsibilities to His family. Even on the cross He was concerned enough about His mother to make arrangements with John to take care of her. Not being conformed to the world certainly does not mean ignoring it.

Being transformed means proving what is the good and acceptable and perfect will of God. If we look at the entire Bible and determine what the will of God is, there are a few realities we can know with certainty. First, it is God's will that all men be saved. Salvation is His will—

> *The Lord is not slack concerning His promise, as some count slackness, but is longsuffering toward us, not willing that any should perish but that all should come to repentance.* (2 Pet. 3:9)

Another major concept is that God wants us to live a right life. We call it righteousness. Understand, however, that righteousness does not mean following a bunch of rules about how you dress or how long your hair is, but rather living with godly attitudes so your life is a reflection of the character of God. It means you do not steal. You are honest. You have integrity. You take on the divine nature of God (Rom. 3:20; 5:19).

A third part of God's perfect will is that He wants His people to experience all the promises He has made to them. Adam and Eve lived in the promises and then lost them. God has been trying to get us back to the promises ever since (Luk. 3:38; Rom. 5:12, 14; 1 Cor. 15:22). Jesus redeemed everything that Adam and Eve gave up when they sinned, and now it is His perfect will that His people live in that redemption.

Adam and Eve experienced promises on earth. And while heavenly blessings are good, you probably don't need to be convinced that you should have them. The earthly blessings are as much a part of God's will as the heavenly ones. There are more Scriptures referencing money, wealth, and prosperity than there are for prayer. That is how important God considers it to be.

What is the perfect will of God? In short, it is these four items:

- get saved
- live right
- build the kingdom
- get rich—prosper

This is where God wants to lead us. How do we get there? We become transformed by changing how we think. We change how we think by filling our minds with the principles of God.

Many years ago God spoke a passage of Scripture to me audibly. He woke me in the middle of the night and spoke to me:

Trust in the Lord with all your heart,
And lean not on your own understanding;
In all your ways acknowledge Him,
And He shall direct your paths. (Prov. 3:5–6)

As we acknowledge God's direction, He will lead us into that which is His perfect will. He will direct us. A literal rendering of this verse from the original Hebrew says that the Lord will straighten out the path of His devoted, faithful servants and make that path prosperous. In the New Testament, the devoted, faithful servants are the ones who multiplied the minas they were given, those who were investors, who put the money to work.

The passage in Proverbs also tells us that God will lead us in the type of action and in the opportunities we should be involved in. The word "acknowledge" suggests that we have an intimacy with God in prayer that conceives and births blessings and victories that direct our paths toward fruitful and life-giving endeavors.

By becoming financially literate, we are not ignoring the importance of spiritual direction or prayer. In fact, we are acknowledging God's will for our lives by doing all that we know how to do, learning how to do more, and listening for God's direction as we go. Direction is not of any use to a person who is not moving. God expects us to do the part that we can. He will do the part that we cannot. If we are not doing our part, He is limited in how much He can do.

No More Excuses

I have said all of this to bring you to a point where you have no excuses left. If you are lacking education, you can read. There is nothing wrong with your brain. If your background is filled with poverty and abuse and sickness, you can overcome it. Others have overcome worse. If you think there is no opportunity for investment, it is only because you have not become financially literate enough to notice opportunities when they are in front of you. They are actually there all the time. If you think the world is against you, God is for you and that is more than enough to push you over the edge to success and wealth. God is waiting for you to do something that He can bless. There is no excuse anymore. Excuses become limiters that turn real dreams into idle wishes.

> Excuses become limiters that turn real dreams into idle wishes.

The time has come to stop making excuses. The most important step most people can make in becoming wealthy is to shut their mouths. When you can start speaking the right things, then open it again. Until then just be quiet. The Word places tremendous importance on what comes out of your mouth: "A fool's mouth is his destruction, and his lips are the snare of his soul" (Prov. 18:7).

This is another way of saying a fool's speech destroys him and his lips are like a noose that strangles the vitality and the desire in his heart. When your speech is negative and junk comes out of your mouth, you destroy your desire and passion to gain wealth. Turn your speech around and begin to speak the Word of God and you will ignite your passion and set your direction.

When Jesus told the parable of the sower in Mark 4:3–20, He identified four kinds of people. The story involves the sowing of seed which is the Word (v. 14). The Word involves the things that we have been discussing, the perfect will of God which is for you to be saved, righteous, and prosperous.

The ground on which the seed falls represents people and how they respond to the Word. The first is the wayside: "And it happened, as he sowed, that some seed fell by the wayside; and the birds of the air came and devoured it" (Mrk. 4:4). Jesus explained that these are people who have the Word stolen away by Satan (v. 15). These are the ones who don't even listen. They shut out the whole idea of God's will for them before they even try it.

The second type of ground is stony ground where there is no depth for the roots to get a hold, and the heat of the day causes the growth to wither away.

These likewise are the ones sown on stony ground who, when they hear the word, immediately receive it with gladness; and they have no root in themselves, and so endure only for a time. Afterward when tribulation or persecution arises for the word's sake, immediately they stumble. (Mrk. 4:16–17)

These are the "I can't" people who get all excited about God's will and prosperity but as soon as they are confronted with the work involved, they suddenly become discouraged and just can't do it anymore. They have gotten some of the concepts but not learned to be financially literate, and so there is no depth to their dreams. They have no root and so they endure only a short time. They don't learn. They just talk and, as things get rough, their talk becomes, "I can't hang on." "I've tried for three weeks and it didn't work." "It's too much work." "I don't have time to study." "I don't have time to learn all of this stuff."

The third kind of ground is that in which the seed begins to grow but gets choked out by weeds.

Now these are the ones sown among thorns; they are the ones who hear the word, and the cares of this world, the deceitfulness of riches, and the desires for other things entering in choke the word and it becomes unfruitful. (Mrk. 4:18–19)

This group is people who can't wait. They have to have things now. "I've got to buy my new car now." "I've got to have a new dress now." "I need a new house now." The concerns for looking prosperous choke out the seed that could actually make them prosperous. They have convinced themselves they can't wait.

The fourth type of ground is that where the seed becomes rooted, grows, and displays a thriving plant. "But these are the ones sown on good ground, those who hear the word, accept it, and bear fruit: some thirty fold, some sixty, and some a hundred" (Mrk. 4:20). This last type represents people who have learned to educate themselves, plant their seed, make investments, and bring in the harvest at the appropriate time. This group took the time to become good ground for the Word of God to grow in and, as a result, they fulfilled His perfect will. These are the good and faithful servants. So what kind of ground are you going to be?

This question brings us back to the matter of what you do with your mouth. To make ground good for planting, it has to be cleared of rocks and weeds, and it has to be plowed. The confession that you develop, the words you constantly speak, will determine what kind of ground you become. It is not far off to say your mouth is the plow that prepares your ground. Learn to use it properly—

A man's stomach shall be satisfied from the fruit of his mouth;
From the produce of his lips he shall be filled.
Death and life are in the power of the tongue,
And those who love it will eat its fruit. (Prov. 18:20–21)

In the Hebrew, this really says that a man's belly or womb or heart shall be increased or satisfied from the production of his speech. The simile of the womb is appropriate for how speech works. When Adam was first created, God recognized that he needed a mate. His mate was Eve, a woman—a "wombed man." She was made that way so she could carry the seed that would produce life. The seed needed time to grow from conception so it could be born. During that time it was nurtured and cared for.

In the New Testament, Mary provided the same kind of illustration of how spiritual seed is conceived and born. By faith, she received in her womb the Word of God, Jesus. The child was nurtured and fed and, in time, the Word was born. He became flesh and dwelled among us.

The concept presented in Proverbs is the same. The fruit of your mouth becomes seed that is planted in the womb of your heart. From that conception it is nurtured and it grows until you give birth to it. If your speech is negative, if it constantly says, "I can't do it, it will never work," then you will be filled with the produce of your lips—poverty and failure. If your speech is constantly the Word of God, then you will be filled with that and fulfill God's perfect will in your life. You will be saved, righteous, and prosperous.

"Death and life are in the power of the tongue, and those who love it will eat its fruit" (Prov. 18:21). This means your tongue can bring either ruin or prosperity. Your belief is fueled by the things your tongue speaks. You are either speaking death, ruin, loss, and poverty or you are speaking life, prosperity, and wealth. What you speak is sown in your heart until it becomes so strong it is birthed into reality. Your speech creates or directs your beliefs and desires. If your speech is right, then your desire will be for all the rewards God has promised.

By putting all these things we have discussed in order—your attitude, your drive or passion, and your speech—you will put yourself in such a position that God can finally do something to really bless you. That's what He wanted to do from the beginning but He has been waiting for you. And now that we have come this far, it is time for some strategies that will enable you to prosper from God's direction as He guides your path. Much of what I share is my own testimony. I'm not bragging . . . just sharing with you some of the things God has taught me over the years that have worked. The more that I leaned on Him instead of my own understanding, the more He has directed my paths.

Wise Strategies

One of the major investments most people make is their house. To buy a house you have to know a little something about real estate and how the market works. Just buying a property doesn't guarantee you will make money. You need to buy smart. You can buy a house and make a few dollars or you can buy smart and make a whole bunch of dollars.

> When you buy a home, you need to look at the least expensive home in the most expensive neighborhood that you can afford.

A new home, a single standing, single dwelling home, will give you the greatest potential for increase of anything most families can do. When you buy a home, you need to look at the least expensive home in the most expensive neighborhood you can afford. The only real reason for buying the most expensive house in the neighborhood is to show off. Get over yourself before it costs you a lot of money. The value per square foot of your home is set by the houses around yours. If your house is the most expensive, then your house will be valued at less than it is actually worth. If yours is the least expensive, it will be valued higher than its actual worth. The greatest profit comes from buying the less expensive house in the more expensive neighborhood.

If you buy a new home early in the production, just as they are starting to lay out the community, and then watch the rest of the community grow up, you will get your house at the lowest possible price for a house built in that area. You might have to put up with some dust and maybe a few nails in the road, but the profit will make it worth it. As the builder continues to build, inflation goes up, the price of the model goes up, and the value of your house continues to grow right along with everything else. By the time the neighborhood is finished, you have been working in your yard and beautifying the yard with starter plants and trees. Four years later they are large and beautiful plants and trees. You may have started with linoleum in the house because that was all you could afford, but you save twenty-five dollars a week until you can put in nice tile in the bathroom. Little by little you steadily improve the house. You keep the yard nice.

By the fifth year of your ownership, the value of the house will peak. If you plan to keep a house for only four or five years and sell it, you will make the most possible money off of it. I am currently living in my eighth house. I only kept one of them for longer than four years. Our boys were in high school and we didn't really want to change schools for them. So we stayed for eight years. When I originally bought the house I paid $99,000. At the end of four years the house would have sold for $160,000. That was the average price of the homes around it. Four years later I sold it for $117,000. During the first four years the house increased in value by $60,000. In the following four years it dropped $43,000. I still made $18,000 over what I had originally paid, but by waiting that extra four years I really gave up more than $40,000 of equity that was potential profit.

I love my home. These houses are where I live, but I have learned to think of them as investments. Because of how I have managed them, I now have $200,000 in equity. By the time I move into my next house, it will be paid for, free and clear.

Your home is an asset if you handle it right. Make sure you buy something that will be profitable. If you buy in an older neighborhood, you will pay premium dollar and probably not get much more out of it than you originally put into it. You really haven't made anything. God can show you the best opportunities. Learn the market and watch for them. Listen to God for His direction.

About a year ago, I was traveling with a couple of friends. We had talked about buying a property in an area where it could be used as a rental. It was a resort area that could prove to be very lucrative. We went there to look, but nothing really worked out. We wanted to buy an inexpensive house or cabin. Then we saw a house that we all fell in love with. It was far more expensive than what we originally had in mind, but as we walked into it we felt the presence of God. Though it looked like there was no way we could get this house, the three of us pooled our resources. We walked around the house and prayed over it. We thanked God for it. We claimed it, based on the anointing that we felt. By a miracle we were able to get the loan and buy the house.

There was some work that needed to be done. Our investment needed some new doors, a little touch-up paint, and some odds and ends. We did these things and put in some new furniture. Now the house is renting for $420 to $480 a night, and it is booked for nearly a year in advance. The income from the property is covering not only the payments on the loan but also an additional $14,000 to $15,000 a month!

Over the first three months that we owned it, the equity on the house also increased tremendously because of the development in the area. It quickly became worth far more than we paid for it. The point to be taken here is that we actually took the time to go and do something. We looked for opportunities for investments.

As we made the effort, we found that God blessed our efforts, gave us direction and confirmation, and made the investment profitable. Was there a risk involved? Yes, there was. Was it a little scary to commit to such a great investment? Yes, it was. Did it stretch me a little? Yes, it did. Was it worth the trouble? Absolutely. God is anxiously waiting for us to take a few risks so He can bless us.

The same principles hold true for buying cars. I bought a new car a couple of times. I saw a car that I liked and I bought it. I also lost some serious money on it. A brand new car drops thousands of dollars in value the moment you drive it off the lot. The best that you can possibly do is to get your money back when you sell it and even that is not likely. You will almost certainly lose money on it.

If you can think of your car as an asset, then you will buy something you can improve and sell for more than you paid for it. There are ways to do this. My son Scot has done it on a regular basis for years. He finds a good deal in the newspaper, fixes it up, buffs it out, steams the engine, makes it look nice, and does whatever odds and ends are required. Then he sells it for $1,000 or $1,500 more than he paid for it.

> If you can think of your car as an asset, then you will buy something you can improve and sell for more than you paid for it.

The direction of God can help you in every purchase you make in life. Everybody buys clothes. They are a necessity. Too often, however, we buy based on emotion. We see a suit or a dress that we just have to have. It might be $400 but we reason that if we don't buy it now it will be gone, so we spend the extra money.

You can go to the most expensive district in town and buy more for less. Or you can go to the poorest district in town and pay less for less. Or you can go to the nicest stores and watch for their fifty- and seventy-percent-off sales. Often you can get $700 suits for $100. You make the effort to shop and God will bring the good deals across your path.

Maureen and I have done this for years. She might see a dress she loves. We claim that dress. It is hers. We have tithed and sown seed, so God is obligated to prosper whatever we touch. We claim the dress so no one else can buy it. Then we leave. A week later we come back and the dress has been marked down. We thank God for the dress and come back a week after that. It is down a little more. We keep coming back until it's down about seventy percent. Then we buy that $400 dress for $129.

This happened to me at a store in a local mall. I saw a buckskin jacket that I wanted. It was glove leather doeskin, the color of actual leather, not dyed, but the natural light color. I tried it on, zipped it up. I loved that coat. I didn't need the coat but I really loved it. The problem was that it was $429. I wasn't going to pay that much for a coat I don't need. But I really liked the coat. So I claimed it. I knew exactly which coat it was because the zipper jammed a little so I could always identify it.

For eleven months I kept coming back and visiting my coat. I sowed seed in the kingdom of God so it was my coat. The price gradually dropped. It went to $350. Then it was down to $250. Then it dropped below $200. I was tempted but I waited a while longer. Every other coat around it sold but that one stayed there. It was my coat. Eleven months after I claimed it, the price dropped to $129 and I bought it.

Many people have their taxes done by a large tax service. You pay money to someone who has no real interest in saving you money. They just want to insure that nothing they do will be audited, which will require them to stay involved at a later time and very likely cost them money. So they will only give you deductions that are assured to attract little or no attention from the IRS. They won't take a chance on anything. It is important to find a tax person who will save you every dollar he can. I'm not advocating anything illegal. If you owe taxes you need to pay them. But there are many legal deductions you can claim if you know what they are. Every dollar you get back is another dollar you can invest.

There are a multitude of things you can do to save or make money. I have a friend who saves coupons. He's been saving them for many years and uses them regularly when shopping. He has told me stories of going into a grocery store and having them owe him money! If you could save twenty-five dollars a week on groceries you would have a substantial amount to invest in a very short time.

> Twenty-five dollars a week can make you a millionaire in thirty years if you don't do anything with it but put it in the bank.

Twenty-five dollars a week can make you a millionaire in thirty years if you don't do anything with it but put it in the bank. Imagine what you could do with it if you learned to invest in stocks. The only thing preventing you from gaining this wealth is you. You have convinced yourself that it is beyond your capability and so you just sit and do nothing. You should just stop talking instead. You might be better off.

Chapter 5 Summary

You Talk Too Much

The problem is not money. It is you. You must accept responsibility for your own attitude. You must prepare yourself to succeed.

You must think differently to act differently, to choose differently, and to succeed differently than you have in the past.

Changing How You Think

Romans 12:1–2 tells us to present our bodies as a living sacrifice, holy and acceptable to God, which is our reasonable service. We are not to be conformed to this world, but transformed by the renewing of our minds.

1. We must be a living sacrifice. Dead people don't bring glory to God.
2. We must be a holy and acceptable sacrifice. We have to have a right heart.
3. We must renew our minds. We have to think differently. We cannot be conformed to the world system of beliefs. The worldly belief system says you will only have enough to get by.

Being transformed means proving what is the good, acceptable, and perfect will of God. What is the perfect will of God?

1. He wants all men to be saved (2 Pet. 3:9).
2. He wants us to be righteous, that is, to reflect the character of God (Rom. 3:20; 5:19).
3. He wants us to experience all the promises He has made to us (Luk. 3:38; Rom. 5:12, 14; 1 Cor. 15:22).
4. He wants us to enjoy the blessings—both spiritual and earthly blessings—that come with the promises.

In other words, the perfect will of God is:

1. Get saved.
2. Live right.
3. Build the kingdom.
4. Get rich and prosper.

The Greatest Obstacle to the Perfect Will of God

The biggest obstacle to attaining the perfect will of God is your mouth. Speak positively and it will fuel your passion. Speak negatively and it will destroy your passion.

The Parable of the Sower (Mrk. 4:3–20) illustrates the different ways we can react to the Word of God.

1. The Wayside—Those who don't listen.
2. Stony Ground—Those who get excited about God's will and prosperity, but as soon as they run into any difficulty, the first thing out of their mouth is, "I can't do it. It's too hard."
3. Weeds—Those who can't wait. They have to have it now and they squander the seed that could make them prosperous.
4. Good Ground—Those who hear the Word, accept it, act on it, and bear fruit.

Your mouth acts as a plow and helps determine what kind of ground you will become. As you speak, so you will be.

Another illustration is the seed planted in the womb. It has to grow and be nurtured and fed before it is finally born.

Strategies for Investment

A house is the biggest investment most people will make.

1. Look for the least expensive house in the most expensive neighborhood you can afford.
2. Buy a home early in the production process, just as the community is starting to develop.
3. Improve the house gradually over time.
4. Plan to sell the house in four to five years, when its value peaks.

Cars

1. Think of your car as an asset.
2. Don't buy new.
3. Look for a car that can be cleaned up and resold for more than you bought it for.

Clothes

1. Watch for sales on quality items. Don't feel that you have to buy it now.

Taxes

1. Don't get your taxes done by a large tax service. Find a tax person who will save you every dollar he can and not just worry about what happens if you get audited.
2. Learn as much about tax laws as you can and apply what you know to your business.

6

You're Brain-Dead

WE ALL HAVE CERTAIN ROUTINES THAT WE FALL INTO. WE TEND TO DO them without thinking too much about them. They become habit. Most of the time they are pretty harmless. For example, when I get ready to leave my house I walk into the garage. I push the garage door button. The garage door goes up. I get in the car and I start backing up. I've done it a thousand times.

The other day, though, Maureen and I walked into the garage and something was different. I pushed the button, got in the car, and started to back up. But the garage door stuck halfway up its tracks. Maureen just happened to look back as the car started to move and I was able to stop just in time. But if she hadn't looked when she did, I would have backed right through the door. I just didn't notice what was going on. The door always went up before. I didn't even have to look at it to know that. I didn't have to look back in order to get out of the garage. I could do it in my sleep. I was essentially brain-dead at that moment.

You may laugh, but we all experience similar lapses of thought. How many times have you nearly backed over your kid's bicycle because you just didn't look? How often have you driven to work and found you couldn't remember anything about the trip? You don't even know for sure that you stopped at a stoplight. How many times have you driven twenty miles past a freeway exit before you realized you weren't in the right place?

Routine and habit have a place in our lives. But there is a lot to be said for awareness. It is amazing how many things we miss every day because we are not aware of our surroundings. Someone gave me a tape about ten years ago that changed my life. It contained a teaching about color codes as they relate to human awareness. It talked about code white, code yellow, code red, and code orange. The ones that are important to our subject are the first two. Code white is when you are not aware at all. You change lanes when someone is there. You walk into people because you didn't see them crossing your path. You're in a world of your own and nothing around you is very real to you. People in code white are the ones who sit in a fast food restaurant when a guy with an Uzi walks in and starts shooting. They just sit there and wait for their turn. The reason is that their minds have shut down. They sit because there isn't enough mental activity happening for them to respond. By the time their brains process the message, "You're about to be shot," it's already too late. Their minds are closed.

That is the world I used to live in. We are all there at least part of the time. It's where I was when I almost backed through the garage door. But there is another place to live. Code yellow means being aware of your surroundings. You begin to notice things happening in the room. When you're driving you see what the guy behind you or beside you is doing. You notice cars in parking lots and side streets that are coming out. You see pedestrians and pets on the sidewalk.

The Power of Awareness

It's not that we are dumb. We are just not aware. The human brain is an incredible thing, an awesome, untapped resource. It is thousands of times faster than any computer known to man. It can store an almost infinite amount of information. You can learn a dozen languages, get seven doctorate degrees, memorize the entire encyclopedia from A to Z, and still only use a tenth of your potential. The brain runs your respiration, digestion, cell growth, hormonal levels—virtually your entire body—and you're not even aware of what's happening. The amazing thing is that you don't have to be aware for the brain to do many of the things that it does. It just does them.

> It's not that we are dumb. We are just not aware.

It is this aspect of how the brain works that actually makes it so fascinating. It is designed to deal with a tremendous amount of information, and it does that by filtering the non-essential information out and ignoring it. Rather than trying to process every piece of sensory input that comes along, your brain, without your awareness, analyzes everything and determines whether you need to know it or not. The filtering process is based mostly on your past experiences.

But your perceptions are colored by your brain's ability to ignore things. Often something that is actually different is perceived by your brain as being just like those things you are familiar with. To illustrate what I am saying, let me describe a study in which various playing cards were flashed on screen for a fraction of a second. People were asked to identify them. It was really very easy to do, but then the researchers began changing the colors of the cards. The subjects began to identify the cards incorrectly because their brains changed the shape of the symbols to fit the colors. When they saw a red four of clubs, for example, they identified it as a four of hearts because they unconsciously knew that clubs are not red. The brain adjusted the perception to fit a known experience.

A conscious effort is required to make our brains pay attention to information that is different from what we are used to. When we live entirely by routine and habit, we stop noticing anything around us. Our brains adjust the information in such a way that we see everything according to our past experience. We see neither dangers nor opportunities. We just sit while the world strolls by and we notice nothing and change nothing. Today looks the same as yesterday did, whether it is or not. We are not aware.

The danger is that our lack of awareness can be a problem since our enemy is always seeking our destruction. The Word of God tells us to be alert. "Be sober, be vigilant; because your adversary the devil walks about like a roaring lion, seeking whom he may devour" (1 Pet. 5:8). It is interesting that the text does not say the devil sneaks around like a silent snake that will bite you without warning. He roars like a lion. If you are in the jungle and you hear a lion roar, you should have enough sense to avoid him.

> If you are in the jungle and you hear a lion roar, you should have enough sense to avoid him.

But if you're brain-dead, you probably won't even pay attention. Your brain will adjust your perception of the roar to fit your normal life and it will just become part of the background noise. The devil gives himself away in so many ways that it is really amazing we ever get caught by him. For someone whose primary weapon is deception, he is awfully blatant.

Peter said to be "sober," which means, "Don't be drunk." That may seem obvious, but it involves more than simply avoiding alcohol. It has to do with being serious about what you are doing.

Be serious and determined. The text also says to be vigilant, to stay awake and be watchful and alert like a sentry on night watch. We don't have to go looking for the devil but we are to be aware of what is going on around us.

The same idea is conveyed in another verse in 1 Peter, "Therefore gird up the loins of your mind, be sober, and rest your hope fully upon the grace that is to be brought to you at the revelation of Jesus Christ" (1:13). "Gird up the loins of your mind" is an old King James expression. The New International Version phrases it this way: "Prepare your minds for action." It means to become alert so you are ready to act. Get your mind thinking. Get it operating because God wants you to be prepared for the hope He has prepared for you. If you are not alert, you will miss it. Your brain can be trained to process input differently. You can be more aware of everything around you. You can learn to notice things.

Paul comments on the importance of knowing the devil's plans—"I have forgiven that one for your sakes in the presence of Christ, lest Satan should take advantage of us; for we are not ignorant of his devices" (2 Cor. 2:10–11).

This word "devices," or "schemes," means we are not ignorant of the perceptions, purposes, or thoughts that he throws in front of us to try and get us to conform to his way of thinking. It is not the obvious things associated with Satan that are a problem to us, things like witchcraft and the occult. It is the subtle attempts he makes to change our perceptions. We are not to be ignorant of his schemes.

Mary and Joseph

Luke 2 describes an incident in which Mary and Joseph had a brain-dead moment. They went to Jerusalem every year to celebrate Passover. It was a part of their regular routine. But when Jesus turned twelve years old, something changed. They didn't really notice the significance of the change at the time, beyond just the normal rituals and sacrifices at the Temple, but Jesus took notice of it. According to Jewish custom, that was the age at which He became an adult. As soon as that happened Jesus began serious preparation for His ministry.

During the Festival of Unleavened Bread, which was technically the week after Passover but in a general sense was considered part of the Passover celebration, it was the custom for the Rabbis and learned men of Judaism to gather in the covered porticos of the outer Temple courtyard and discuss the Scriptures, teaching and debating as they talked. It was a marvelous opportunity for anyone in Jerusalem to sit and listen to the greatest wisdom and spiritual insight of the land, asking questions and commenting. As Jesus was now an adult, He thought it appropriate that He join in that discussion in order to learn as much as He could learn in preparation for the ministry He knew was coming.

There are a couple of things we can learn from this account. The first is that Jesus was clearly committed to using His mind and educating Himself for the future. Most of us use our brains for entertainment. Since 1960, the education level of Americans has deteriorated tremendously. The average reading level of incoming college freshmen is down to about a fifth-grade level. The problem is that we use our brains for entertainment, not for learning. We watch television and our brains shut down. There are studies that show mental activity drops to almost nothing when people watch television, even when the program is educational. We actually limit our awareness by our activities.

Jesus, however, was not entertaining Himself. As soon as He reached adulthood He was in the midst of the most educated men in the country and learning everything He could learn that would help Him fulfill His destiny. He got His brain working, preparing it for action.

Our perception of this incident has been that He was the Son of God who came into the Temple at the age of twelve and began teaching, but that was not the situation. He was there to learn, and they were impressed with His level of understanding. He asked questions, made comments, and gave answers to their questions that demonstrated He was not waiting until He was thirty to prepare.

This story also tells us Jesus was aware of His surroundings. He knew He was stepping into adulthood. He saw the teaching of the learned men and acted to take advantage of the opportunity to learn. He paid attention to what was going on around Him. His mind was working. Mary and Joseph, on the other hand, were brain-dead. They were following the same routine they had followed for years. They just assumed Jesus was with them when they left town. It took them a whole day to notice anything was wrong.

When they had finished the days, as they returned, the Boy Jesus lingered behind in Jerusalem. And Joseph and His mother did not know it; but supposing Him to have been in the company, they went a day's journey, and sought Him among their relatives and acquaintances. So when they did not find Him, they returned to Jerusalem, seeking Him. (Luk. 2:43–45)

It's not hard to understand how this happened. They had many friends and relatives in the group they were traveling with and Jesus was a well-behaved son who could be expected to do what was right in any circumstance. So they could easily just assume He was there somewhere in the traveling party. But the routine of twelve years lulled them to sleep and they failed to notice the significance of the Son of God becoming an adult. They missed the opportunity. In fact they missed it so much that even after they found Him, three days later, they still failed to see what was happening.

So when they saw Him, they were amazed; and His mother said to Him, "Son, why have You done this to us? Look, Your father

and I have sought You anxiously." And He said to them, "Why did
you seek Me? Did you not know that I must be about My Father's
business?" But they did not understand the statement which He
spoke to them. (Luk. 2:48–50)

Being brain-dead carries a double danger. When we are locked
into habitual thinking patterns, we fail to see the enemy's attacks
coming, even though he is roaring, and we likewise fail to see opportunities, even when they are right in front of us. Our perceptions are limited.

Unfortunately, it is not easy to change perceptions. It requires
a distinct effort. It requires education. This is one of the reasons
it is so important to become financially literate. The perceptions
that you have were formed from your childhood and it will take
some doing to alter them. It is a characteristic of human beings
that it takes only an ounce of information to form a perception,
but a ton of information to change it.

By this time, your perceptions should be changing. You should
be starting to see the possibilities that God has in mind for you.
You ought to have a new perspective on wealth and poverty. The
devil should no longer be able to deceive you into believing that
you should be poor or that you can't be wealthy.

Another statement Jesus made highlights the manner in
which Satan works: "The thief does not come except to steal, and
to kill, and to destroy. I have come that they may have life, and
that they may have it more abundantly" (John 10:10). Life comes
as a result of salvation. Abundant life comes when we begin to
live in the promises of God, experiencing all of the blessings He
wants us to experience. It means having everything God intended
for us.

The thief has in mind stealing and killing. The Greek word
used here for "steal" means exactly the same thing as the English
word. The thief wants to take away from you all that God wants to
give you. "Kill" has a little different nuance in Greek than it does

in English, however. It does not simply mean kill in the sense of killing people. The word translates best as "blows smoke." The devil blows smoke or fog. He puts up a screen that gets you to believe a lie. If you believe the lie, then you will put your faith in the world's system and you will accept sickness and poverty.

One perception that the church has bought into concerning the wealthy is that they are not really spiritual. They come to church and drop money in the offering plate, but they are second-class citizens of the kingdom of God because they spend so much of their time dealing with money. The more "spiritual" people spend their time studying the Bible, praying, prophesying, and doing miracles. That cold-shoulder attitude has caused many wealthy people to feel put down and inferior and even driven them out of the church. The devil has stolen them and stolen the finances that should have been keeping ministries operating.

> If you train yourself to become aware and get your brain working and ready for action, then you will see Satan's schemes and you will know how to avoid them.

If you train yourself to become aware and get your brain working and ready for action, then you will see Satan's schemes and you will know how to avoid them. You will stop believing the lie and you will start to see opportunities for all kinds of investments. It all hinges on how badly you want to become financially literate. I have said all of this to get to a simple statement—there are opportunities to make money showing up every day. If you are aware of your surroundings, you will see them and you will also recognize when the devil is trying to steal them from you.

Taking Action

Here are a few thoughts about finances that might help you in gaining a biblical perspective. Infuse your thinking with them and you will start to see the world of money a little differently.

Lee Iacocca said that the trick is to make sure you don't die waiting for prosperity to come. "Waiting" is a key word in that statement. If you are waiting, then you're not doing anything, and if you're not doing anything, then you're not gaining wealth. You're just waiting. Stop waiting and do something. Thousands of people are brought into poverty by their great anxiety not to be thought of as poor. Stop worrying about what you don't have and do something with what you do have. If you are brain-dead, do something about it. Get your mind ready for action. Become financially literate.

When we talk about finances, most people are so brain-dead, so unaware, they don't even know their current financial status. That is why we began this book by talking about the importance of determining your financial worth. You need to understand where you are. A significant step toward awareness is the simple act of making a budget and sticking to it. The following is a budget plan I have been using for years. By following it you will know every day what you have available to spend and you will never be taken by surprise at the end of the month by too many bills you can't pay. It is really quite simple.

The first step is to determine a few guidelines for how you deal with bills. Do not pay bills the instant they come in. Plan a monthly pay date as you set up accounts. The thirtieth of the month is best. When you enter agreements for payments for electric, rent, water, gas, and so on, ask for a due date of the thirtieth of the month. If you haven't already done this, call or write a request to make the due date the thirtieth of the month.

Set up two checking accounts and one savings account. The first checking account is to be used exclusively for bills. You never write any other check out of it. The second account is for everyday expenses. The savings account is to use as a backup. You should build up a reserve in it sufficient to cover three months of expenses. In order to do that, put an automatic pay to your savings account every week of at least twenty dollars.

Figure out your total fixed and semi-fixed expenses each month. Add up your tithe, rent or mortgage, car payments, auto insurance, utilities, credit card payments, and anything else that requires a regular monthly check. Every time you get a paycheck, make a deposit into the checking account that is exclusively for bills. If you get paid every week, then the deposit should be one fourth the total of your monthly bills. If you are paid every two weeks or twice a month then the deposit should be one half of your total expenses. That way, at the end of the month, you will have enough money there to cover all of your bills.

It is important to remember that money put into this account is not yours. It is already spent. Never carry this checkbook with you anywhere. Write only the monthly bills out of it.

The amount remaining each month, after the deposits are made into the first checking account, is what you have left over. That is not necessarily extra money, however. It is for the weekly expenses such as food, gasoline, clothing, entertainment, and your savings deposit.

Any remaining amount after that lets you increase debt expense or save more, but if there is too little left for food, gas, entertainment, and clothing, you have a problem that can only be solved by cutting your expenses or increasing your income. If you have a surplus left, then you can choose to upgrade your lifestyle, save more, purchase something or, the option I would recommend, start investing in your future. As you study and learn more about how money works and as you train yourself to look for opportunities, you will find them. Many are available every day. Most people just don't think enough about it to figure them out.

I believe real estate is a good investment. At the time of this writing, property values in the Phoenix area are up to about $150,000 an acre. We bought the property that Living Word Bible Church sits on for $40,000 an acre. That gives you an idea of how much the value can increase in only a couple of years if you learn to buy in the right location. Houses and property will continue to increase in value. They are a good investment.

But you might be worried about going that far in debt. You need to understand that if you can sell your house for more than you owe on it, then it is not a debt, but an asset. That makes real estate a good investment.

The stock market is also a good investment. It can be risky, especially if you have not educated yourself in how it works, but the stock market has generally gone up year after year. There are dips in stock prices. We had the crash of 1929 and the crash of 1987 and then there were some problems in 1992. But in spite of those kinds of things, if you had put money in the stock market fifty years ago and left it alone, it would have multiplied many times over along the way. Over a period of time, the market has always gone up.

> Over a period of time, the market has always gone up.

The problem most people have with the stock market is that they panic at the wrong times. The market drops so they get scared and sell everything at a low price. The rich, who didn't panic, buy up what you sold at a low price and wait for the market to go back up. That's how the rich get richer.

Which stocks should you buy? Look at companies that are profitable. If the company is making money, you will make money. The shakier the company, the more risk you take with their stock. Generally speaking, the greater the risk, the greater the profits you can make if the company succeeds. There is always risk in investments, but if you learn the market you can invest smart and maximize the opportunity for profit.

Another excellent investment is a 401(k). Many businesses are using them for their employees. If you can start one, you should put as much into it as you can, simply because your company has to match part of what you put in. It is also tax sheltered, which is an advantage.

Most 401(k)s are in mutual funds. These are funds where a whole bunch of people pool their money together to invest in diverse stocks. They average it all together and share the profits.

There are also bonds that you can purchase. We issued bonds at Living Word as a part of the building program. Essentially, those who bought them were loaning money to the church for a period of time in return for a certain amount of interest. The amount of profit can vary depending on the type of bond. They are relatively safe investments.

These types of investments are nothing new. They have been around for a long time. We discussed the parable of the minas in chapter 2. We saw that the good and faithful servants invested their money and doubled it. But where did they invest it?

The details are not given in the Gospels, but from history, we do know some of the investment options available to them. In the early Roman Empire, the government raised money by selling contract bonds and taxation bonds. In other words, you could invest money in the government and earn dividends on your stock. This was happening before Jesus was born and it continued long afterwards. The servants in the parable took money and invested it in what could be considered the world system. The opportunities were available to anyone with the initiative and awareness to notice them and take advantage of them.

The stock market, as we know it today, is not all that new either. The claim for the oldest market goes to Amsterdam—it started in 1531. It is now one of the one hundred and fifty stock markets in existence today.[1] Throughout history, the wealthy got that way in the same manner that they do today. They invested. They watched for opportunities and took a calculated risk based on their knowledge of how money works.

Most Americans have heard of the British East India Company. It was formed in 1602 and began to buy spices, teas, and other goods from the Far East. It was some of that tea that our forefathers made immortal at the Boston Tea Party. That might be considered a setback, but those who invested in the company when it started multiplied their money 143 times.

In 1789, the United States government had just emerged from the Revolutionary War and was completely broke. To raise some capital, it sold eighty million dollars worth of government bonds. The government desperately needed money and those who were aware could invest in the government and earn substantial dividends.[2]

The men who sold these bonds were called broachers. The term originally referred to those who broached or tapped a keg of wine. They punched a hole in the keg so that its contents could be poured out. The government broachers were tapping the finances of the people and bringing them into the government. In time the "a" was dropped from the name and they became known as "brokers."

These broachers worked largely in the capital, which was in New York at that time. To avoid inclement weather, they often worked out of a place called the Turvine Café. This gathering was the beginning of what came to be known as the New York Stock Exchange. The café was located on a little four block street called Wall Street. When the Dutch first settled New York in 1644, they put brush wood around their compound to keep cattle in and Indians out. The governor later built a nine foot high wall, turning the area into a fortress. The street that ran along the wall became know as Wall Street.[3]

I mention this little bit of history because it shows that there have always been opportunities for investments and there have always been investors. There is no reason why you cannot be one. What sets them apart from the poor is their awareness of opportunity. They keep their minds active and ready for action. They are alert and vigilant.

Chapter 6 Summary

You're Brain-Dead

We are usually not very aware of our surroundings. We get into habits and routines and we filter out all kinds of information that isn't immediately relevant.

1 Peter 5:8 tells us to be sober and vigilant. We are to be aware of the enemy's schemes against us so that they do not take us by surprise. When we become locked into habitual thinking patterns, two things happen:

1. We fail to see the enemy's attacks coming.
2. We fail to see opportunities when they are right in front of us.

Changing your perceptions will require some effort. It is characteristic of human beings that it takes only an ounce of information to form a perception, but a ton of information to change it.

There are opportunities to make money showing up every day. If you are aware of your surroundings, you will see them. If you see them, you can act on them.

A Simple Budget Plan

Awareness of your current financial situation is vital. To be aware, you should start a budget and stick to it.

1. Set up your accounts so that you always pay all your bills on the same day each month.

2. Set up two checking accounts and a savings account.
   a. One checking account is exclusively for paying your monthly bills.
   b. The second account is for everyday expenses.
   c. Build a reserve in the savings account large enough to cover three months of bills.
3. Figure your total fixed and semi-fixed expenses.
4. Compute how much of each paycheck is necessary to cover those expenses and deposit that amount into your bills account. That money is not available to you for anything else.
5. Whatever is left over is what you have for food, entertainment, etc. Set aside a portion of it for investment.

Investment Opportunities

Nothing is guaranteed, but there are some investments that have always been relatively good.

1. Real estate, if you buy smart, will usually increase in value over time.
2. Stocks can be risky in the short term, but in the long run, the stock market has always gone up.
3. A 401(k) plan is a good investment for those whose employer offers it.
4. Bonds.

Be aware and opportunities will always present themselves.

7

Self-Control

For several months, I went to the gym with a man from the church. As an expert in nutrition and exercise, he worked out a program for me to accomplish some specific goals. I wanted to build up my body, especially my shoulders. Not everything built up quite the way I wanted it to. We arrived for the first workout. He set the weight on one of the machines and said, "Okay, do twelve reps at this weight." I did twelve and thought to myself, This body building thing is pretty awesome.

I felt great. I was ready for another twelve, but then he increased the weight. Suddenly it wasn't so easy. In fact, it started to hurt a little. Actually, it hurt a lot.

I complained, "I can't do twelve at this weight."

He replied, "Do as many as you can."

"Can't we go back to the other weight? It was easy."

He stared at me mercilessly and said, "No pain, no gain. If you don't experience some pain, you'll never gain any muscle."

"Why would anyone come back and keep doing this week after week?" I wondered. "I'm not that badly out of shape."

The answer? Self-discipline. When you can see the goal clearly in your mind, then the pain is worth it. It is a step on the way to success. But to build muscle, you have to work out on a regular basis, whether it feels good or not. That is self-discipline. We all have choices to make in life. Paul encouraged the Corinthians to make choices that would help them achieve something.

Do you not know that those who run in a race all run, but one receives the prize? Run in such a way that you may obtain it. And everyone who competes for the prize is temperate in all things. Now they do it to obtain a perishable crown, but we for an imperishable crown. (1 Cor. 9:24–25)

We have addressed several concepts already that relate to this verse as it regards wealth. First of all, if you are going to win the prize, you have to run in the race. Most Christians are just watching on the sidelines, cheering when someone running the race fails. They won't even take the chance. But the one certain thing is that if you are not in the race, you will not win the prize. That is the first step. Get in the race.

> If you are going to win the prize, you have to run in the race.

But if you are going to run the race at all, then you must run to win. You are going to have to run harder and longer than you probably ever thought you could. You will have to endure pain and you will have to give up time and energy if you want to achieve success. If you ask an Olympian how long it takes to run a marathon, he will tell you that it is a lot more than running the race itself, a distance just over twenty-six miles. It involves running thousands of miles in preparation just to be able to finish. To actually win takes even greater dedication.

Paul says that those who compete must be "temperate."

That means "in strict training." They forego some comforts in order to train so that they can compete effectively for the prize.

Diets and diet books are a three billion-dollar market in America. You can't go through the store line without being confronted by a new diet program that promises you will lose a hundred pounds in a few days. The problem with diets is that there are none that work effectively in the long term. You may lose a lot of weight, but you will gain it all back as soon as you are finished with the diet if you don't take to heart the lessons learned during the weight loss.

There is no substitute for taking personal responsibility for your eating and exercise habits and learning self-control. Most of us would like to have a pastor lay hands on us and deliver us from chocolate cake. It's not going to happen that way. Self-control means learning to say no. There is no way around it. It is called "self-control" because it involves the "control" of "self." If you don't do it yourself, then it isn't going to happen.

> There is no substitute for taking personal responsibility.

The most basic step in financial self-control is creating a budget. We already looked at a very workable budget. I have used it for many years. But if you make a budget and then ignore it, you will never get anywhere. It does no good to know you can spend only ten dollars when you go ahead and spend fifteen anyway. In this part of our study we are looking for money to invest. The best thing you can do is to develop self-control in the small things. The tendency for most people is to spend money simply because they have it. It makes them feel good to be able to spend it, so they do. Of course that means the money is not available to invest.

It doesn't take much to find this money. If you give up one soda each day, seven days a week, at the end of a year you will have $365 to invest. If you invest it for thirty years at twelve percent interest you will be a millionaire. You could be wealthy at a cost of a single soda a day. But most don't have enough self-control to avoid buying the soda in the first place, so they never have anything to invest.

Self-control is a fruit of the Spirit. It is significant that it is mentioned last, since none of the other fruits can be experienced without it. "But the fruit of the Spirit is love, joy, peace, long-suffering, kindness, goodness, faithfulness, gentleness, self-control. Against such there is no law" (Gal. 5:22–23). Understand that there is a difference between "gifts" of the Spirit and "fruit" of the Spirit. Gifts are absolutely free. When you receive the fullness of the Holy Spirit, you obtain the fullness of all His gifts, freely given to you.

When you first stepped out in the exercise of your gifts, however, it is very likely that you were a little bit flaky. You may have given a word of prophecy that didn't seem to have the impact that you thought it should. But it was given without the tempering quality of love or longsuffering or kindness or gentleness or self-control. Those elements had not grown in you yet.

A gift is received. You simply take it and it is yours. But that doesn't mean you know what to do with it. Fruit has to grow and that takes time. You have to water it and nurture it.

Paul's whole reason for describing the gifts of the Spirit to the church in Corinth was to make sure that they were exercised for "the profit of all" (1 Cor. 12:7). The church there was very busy being "spiritual," but without any concern for the purpose of the gifts. They did not realize self-control was an important part of the whole process. All gifts of the Spirit are subject to the control of the person who has the gift: "And the spirits of the prophets are subject to the prophets" (1 Cor. 14:32).

It is not enough just to be spiritual. Self-control is vital. As you grow into self-control, you will grow into the ability to love unconditionally all of the time. You will learn to have patience. You will learn to have joy. You will be able to operate in longsuffering and perseverance and kindness and gentleness. All these fruits require self-control to be utilized effectively. With self-control, you will flow with the Spirit and the gifts will be beneficial.

Developing Self-Control

The important point I am making is that self-control is a learned behavior. You cannot be delivered into self-control. You have to grow into it. You also have to make an effort to develop it.

I have a problem with chocolate. I love chocolate—cake, fudge, M&M's. There is an area in which I don't have to exercise self-control. It is between the weight of 184 pounds and 194. When I hit 194, I have to impose some self-control. When I get back to 184 then I can relax that control a little. The point is that if I don't make an effort, then I will just keep gaining weight. It doesn't disappear just because I pray over my food.

It is an amazing statistic that seventy percent of the population of America is overweight. That means that at least seven out of every ten people are struggling with self-control. Most of the rest are probably smoking and drinking so much they couldn't gain weight no matter how much they ate. Sixty-nine to seventy percent of the young people of America smoke. Just the fact that so many, both young people and adults, continue to smoke, even though they know it is doing irreparable harm to their lungs and their health, indicates how great the struggle is in our culture. This issue of self-control is extremely important in our lives.

When we see a six-year-old shoot another child, we know there is a problem in society with self-control. The anger rose up, and instead of dealing with whatever made him angry, he just pulled out a gun. There is no self-control. The emptier the pot, the quicker the boil. The less character there is in the child, the faster he loses control.

I see children in the grocery store or toy store who zero in on a toy or candy they want. They cry and scream until the parents cave in; these parents get them anything they ask for just to keep the kids quiet. As soon as they do, they lose the opportunity to teach their child self-control. Self-control says, "You will wait until later. You might get it tomorrow. You might get it next week. In the meantime, appropriate discipline will help you learn to control yourself. When you get done crying, we will discuss the possibility of getting what you want next time. If you ask politely and don't get upset when I say no, then maybe next time you will get it."

Self-control is a learned behavior. It can be one of the very first things a child is taught. When a child cries during the night, there can be several valid reasons. He might need to be fed or changed, for example. But you don't have to jump at the very first sound of his voice. And when the basic needs are taken care of, then it is time to teach self-control. If he just won't sleep all night, there comes a point where you should just let him cry all night. Just close the door. It will help the child develop self-control. If you don't do it, he'll have to eat in the middle of the night for the rest of his life.

> We have a responsibility to teach our children self-control.

We have a responsibility to teach our children self-control. Our son, Scot, began sleeping through the night at the age of six weeks. He was healthy. He was happy. We fed him. We changed his diaper. Everything was fine. We went to bed. He didn't sleep at all the first night. The second night he slept great. He learned self-control at an early age.

Appetites of the Flesh

Self-control has its basis in controlling the appetites of the flesh. We could devote the entire book to misconceptions of what this means. Early in the history of the church, there developed a belief that denying the appetites of the flesh meant moving to the desert, praying constantly, and starving oneself. Husbands and wives were encouraged to separate from each other to avoid all manner of physical contact.

This is not what is meant by controlling the appetites of the flesh. An extensive study of this aspect of church history would show that such attitudes did not derive from the Bible, but from the influences of Greek philosophy and pagan beliefs. A monk in the desert might have the appearance of spirituality, but he will never affect the world since he never talks to anyone, never shares the Gospel with anyone, never does anything that could influence anything in the world for good. Jesus never intended for His people to hide from the world, rendering themselves useless in the building of His kingdom. He told them to go "into" the world (Mrk. 16:15).

What are the appetites of the flesh, then? We can get some insight by looking in the same passage of Scripture where we found the fruit of the Spirit,

> *Now the works of the flesh are evident, which are: adultery, fornication, uncleanness, lewdness, idolatry, sorcery, hatred, contentions, jealousies, outbursts of wrath, selfish ambitions, dissensions, heresies, envy, murders, drunkenness, revelries, and the like, of which I tell you beforehand, just as I also told you in time past, that those who practice such things will not inherit the kingdom of God.* (Gal. 5:19–21)

Let's look at what some of these words mean. *Adultery* means exactly that. It involves unfaithfulness and a failure to honor commitments in the most important relationship in life apart from that with God, your marriage. *Fornication* actually means prostitution—to be prostituted or to be involved in prostitution. It also includes incest. As with adultery, there is a violation of commitments and trust in family relationships. *Uncleanness* means to have impure thoughts of the heart. This is more than just the thoughts that occasionally flash through your brain. The enemy loves to throw them in there, but you don't have to receive them. *Uncleanness* refers to those impure thoughts that you take into your heart and dwell on. *Lewdness* means a loose sexual life or any of the vices that involve the abuse of your body, such as drugs, alcohol, or even excesses of food that are not appropriate.

Idolatry occurs any time things become more important than God. These can be whatever we allow to consume our attention. God wants you to be wealthy but you can make money into an idol. That is why you must keep your attitude right. The word *sorcery* makes us think of witches and the occult, but it really means something very different. It means drug inducing pharmaceuticals. It refers to a craving for any substance that creates a euphoric high. There are natural things you can take that can be good for you, but our society relies heavily on other things. If you have to take one pill to sleep and another pill to wake up, there may be a problem with the appetites of the flesh.

Hatred refers to hostility to man. It includes *contention* and a quarrelsome attitude. If you are constantly quarreling with people, even when they are always wrong, then something of the love and peace that should be yours is missing. *Jealousy* means *envying* other people for what they have. God wants His people to be happy for the prosperity of others. *Wrath* is fierce, uncontrolled anger. It implies any anger that draws you into sin. James comments on selfish ambition when he points out that it is tied to confusion and every evil work (James 3:16). *Dissension* results from those who bring division or provoke division between two people or between friends. *Heresy* means disunity; another definition would be attempting to draw people to oneself instead of drawing them to Christ. *Murder* is fairly self-explanatory. It involves the taking of another life, though there are ways you can take someone's life without killing them. You can murder their reputation, for example, by creating or promoting destructive rumors about them. *Drunkenness* refers to intoxication. *Revelry* means letting loose and raising hell or just having a wild time.

All of these things are desires or appetites of the flesh. It is interesting that they all have one specific thing in common: They result from a lack of self-control. We justify many of them by claiming they are out of our control. Many who commit adultery cite circumstances as their defense. They were "in love" and couldn't help themselves. Many who become addicted to prescription drugs got that way because they didn't think they could sleep without them. Many who lose their temper really believe that if other people were more reasonable, then they wouldn't have to get angry.

In every case the thing that is missing is self-control. The ability to say no to the desires or inclinations of the flesh is the answer to most problems people have. It can be learned. Whenever something wells up inside of us that is not "love, joy, peace, longsuffering, kindness, goodness, faithfulness, gentleness, or self-control," we can say no to it. There is great power in that word, "No." Saying no to Jesus has the power to send you to hell. Saying no to the appetites of the flesh has the power to bring you great blessing.

Self-Control and Wealth

Everything I have said about self-control relates to virtually every area of your life. When we focus on gaining wealth, it becomes obvious that self-control is the one characteristic that will make all of the other things work. We have seen the importance of developing the right attitude toward money. We have made an effort to develop passion. We have dealt with the failures of the past. We have learned to speak the right things. We have gained financial literacy and learned to look for opportunities. But without self-control, we will waste all of that progress. It still comes down to actually doing something with what we have.

When we looked at the parable of the sower in Mark 4, we saw various levels of self-control represented. The first seed fell by the wayside. This is the twenty-five percent of the church who

> It still comes down to actually doing something with what we have.

don't have enough initiative to even get started. There is always an excuse. Such an attitude will stop the Word from working. "I don't have any money." "I don't have any time." "I don't have any means of doing this." "I can't even buy the books." The seed is stolen away before it has a chance to take root.

What you need, if this describes you, is self-control. We already saw that a dollar a day will make you a millionaire if you invest it. You could find a little time to do something to better your position, perhaps by turning off the TV. If you are already working all the time, then you have to learn to work smarter. The opportunities are always there if you look for them. Even if you can't afford the books to make yourself financially literate, you can still find them in the library. They're free there. There really is no excuse.

The second twenty-five percent are hard ground where the seed starts to grow but can't get deep enough to take root, and it withers away. These are people who have made up their minds that it can't be done. They don't have enough self-control to develop any depth. Instead, they seek comfort over success. They just want to drift through life, get their cabin in Glory Land, and not have to deal with too much. They have the potential for prosperity. It is in front of them but they will not exercise the self-control necessary to become productive.

The third type of person is the thorny ground where weeds grow up and choke out the seed. I believe this is where most

Christians live today. There are three things that make the seed unfruitful in them—"the cares of this world, the deceitfulness of riches, and the desires for other things" (Mrk. 4:19).

The cares of the world are distractions that keep them from making the most basic investments. Instead of bringing tithes and offerings into the storehouse, they take the money and spend it on other things they feel they can't live without. When you make the decision to begin tithing, the enemy will challenge you to see if you are really going to do it. The first year that Maureen and I tithed was the most financially difficult year of my life. It takes self-control to keep at it. But you can't be fruitful if you're not tithing into the kingdom of God. You need that to enable God to rebuke the devourer on your behalf.

The second part of this is the deceitfulness of riches. The Greek words used here actually mean to create a delusion, to cheat at wealth, that is, to appear to have money when you actually don't. In other words, buying on credit so that you look like you are rich, even though you still owe on it, is the deceitfulness of wealth. If we had self-control, we would say no to buying liabilities and save the money to invest in assets, even if it meant looking a little poorer. Self-control means delaying the purchase of things we don't really need until we can afford them without going into debt. A little of this self-control will go a long way in finding money to invest.

The third part is the desire for other things. This does not mean that we should not ever desire anything material. God said in Psalm 37:4, "Delight yourself also in the Lord, and He shall give you the desires of your heart." The problem is in why we desire things. You may recall that Hebrew poetry uses two statements set side by side. We looked at a verse in Proverbs that was *antithetical parallelism*, a negative statement and a positive statement. This verse in Psalms is another type of construction, called *synonymous parallelism*. It has two positive statements joined together, and you cannot just take the second line of the verse without paying attention to the first. We must remember to keep our delight in the Lord in order to receive the desires of our hearts.

The desire for other things implies that you are not delighting yourself in God. This is perhaps the most dangerous position of all. It carries much of the same implication as the deceitfulness of riches. It is amazing how much power the desire for things can have. When you truly set your heart on something, such as a new car or clothes, it is only a matter of time before you will have it. You will dwell on it until you find a way to get it.

This is what makes such desires unfruitful. They turn your focus away from delighting in God. Your attention becomes so focused on the thing you want that you will put yourself in debt in order to have it. You will fall for the concept of buying now and paying later. As a result, you end up with credit cards full and monthly payments that include so much interest you have no money left to invest in assets. You are unable to produce anything. That is the whole reason credit cards were invented.

When your desire is to build the kingdom of God, you will recognize that debt is a hindrance to your productivity. You will not let the desire for things choke out the Word. You become like the last twenty-five percent of the seed that fell on good ground. It produced thirty, sixty and a hundredfold. These are the people who learn to exercise self-control so they can wait to buy things until they can actually pay for them. Consequently they have money available to invest, and their money begins to multiply.

Matthew 6:21 is another verse we are quite familiar with, "For where your treasure is, there your heart will be also." In other words, if we expand the meaning of the Greek words, it is saying that in the place where your wealth or deposit is, your heart will also be there. The heart, in Greek, represents the center of the thoughts, passions, affections, and desires. This verse is saying that your heart, thoughts, feelings, and mind will move to focus their energy on that place. It becomes a cumulative force to produce something.

Your heart and your treasure cannot be separated. Your heart will follow your treasure and your treasure will produce the desire of your heart. When you set your heart on something, then it will not be

> God will bless your efforts when you do it His way, but He won't make you do it.

long before your treasure becomes applied to obtaining it. You will begin to use your available treasure to produce the desire. If your heart is set on the kingdom of God, then your treasure will become applied to producing it. It will put you in a

place where God can bless you and multiply your treasure. You will find a cumulative force in your life producing the things you want.

The key to setting all of these things in motion is self-control. No one will force you to get rich. God will bless your efforts when you do it His way, but He won't make you do it. You must learn self-control in order to get there.

Putting Self-Control to Work

All of the financial advice in the world is useless if you do not learn to exercise self-control. When you do, you can begin to make wise financial decisions and carry through with them. You can make profitable investments and see your money multiply. The following suggestions will help you get started but you need the self-discipline first if you are to reach financial independence:

- Open an IRA or 401(k) account if you don't already have one. If you do have one, do your best to invest the maximum amount you are allowed. This reduces your taxes and increases capital. It is a means of reducing liabilities and building assets.
- Start now to keep records of deductible expenses for this year so you will be able to use the long form for your taxes. Study so that you know what is deductible, and then choose a tax

person to do your taxes who is not part of a national chain. Consider investing in the computer program TurboTax.

- If your company has profit sharing or stock purchase programs, begin buying what you can. This will also help you build assets.
- Build a cash cushion for emergencies or "what-ifs." Your savings should contain enough to cover three months of bare minimum living expenses—mortgage, car payment, utilities, and so on.
- Be sure you have an up-to-date will.
- Life insurance programs should be term, not universal life. Those that are front-loaded, meaning the expense charges are deducted early in the policy, or rear-loaded, meaning most of the expense charges occur when the policy is surrendered or cash is withdrawn, do not produce much in the long term. There are better places to invest your money.
- Keep up with money and stock news, that is, the things that affect the money market.
- Be sure to give. Tithes and offerings brought into the storehouse help lower your taxes, since they are deductible. More important, God is obligated to protect your stuff. Offerings become seeds planted into the kingdom. Therefore, whatever your hands touch in the way of investments or labor will produce thirty, sixty, or a hundredfold.
- Study and become financially literate. There is much to be learned. Only when you feel confident, start investing in stocks, bonds, or real estate. Find out about living trusts.
- Get on a budget and hold fast. Reduce expenses. Stop producing more liabilities and build your assets.

All of these activities require a high degree of self-control. If you ever want to accomplish anything, you must develop this quality. There is no way to get around it. There is no shortcut to avoid it. You must have self-control.

Chapter 7 Summary

Self-Control

Financial self-control starts with a budget. It does no good to make a budget, however, if you don't stick to it. You must have self-control.

Developing self-control will enable you to find money to invest. It doesn't take much. If you give up one soda each day, at the end of a year, you will have $365 to invest. If you invest it for thirty years at twelve percent interest, you will be a millionaire.

Self-control is learned behavior. It involves saying, "No," to the appetites of the flesh. Examples of these are in Galatians 5:19–21—adultery, fornication, uncleanness, lewdness, idolatry, sorcery, hatred, contentions, jealousies, outbursts of wrath, selfish ambitions, dissensions, heresies, envy, murders, drunkenness, revelries. They all result from a lack of self-control.

Degrees of Self-Control

The Parable of the Sower represented different degrees of self-control.

1. The Wayside: Those who lack the self-control to even get started.
2. Rocky Soil: Those who have made up their minds that it can't be done. They don't have enough self-control to develop any depth.
3. Weeds: They are made unfruitful by three things:

    a. Cares of the world: Distractions that keep them from making the most basic investments, things they feel they can't live without, but which don't bring them any real benefit.

    b. The deceitfulness of riches: The desire to go into debt to buy thing that make them look rich, even when they're not.

    c. The desire for other things: Delighting in material possessions rather than delighting in God.

4. Good Soil: People who learn to exercise self-control so they can wait to buy things until they can actually pay for them.

Your Heart and Your Treasure

Matthew 6:21 tells us that where your treasure is, there your heart will be also. You cannot separate the two. Where you place your treasure, your heart will follow, and it will produce the desires of your heart.

8

What, Me Work?

A COUPLE OF YEARS AGO I SPOKE AT A CHURCH THAT WAS ABOUT FIVE years old. The pastor was a good man who worked very diligently at his ministry. The church was relatively small so he held down a full-time job in addition to the work of pastoring. He was conscientious and hard-working.

But he never had any fun. The ministry became drudgery, a heavy burden that he faithfully carried day after day, week after week. I looked him in the eye and said, "You need to have some fun. Let's go play golf." He expected to spend the day in spiritual pursuits, praying and studying, preparing for the service the next day. He didn't know how to play golf anyway. I deflected his excuses. "I've already prayed. I've already studied. I'm ready to preach right now. If I'm ready to preach and I'm all prayed up, we can play golf. I'll teach you how."

We headed to the golf course and by the third hole he was having so much fun he forgot all about how difficult the ministry was. The next day his wife joined us and started to have fun too. It didn't seem to hurt their ministry any since the church has grown so much since then that he is no longer forced to work his second job. Everything in his church that he touches is prospering.

A good work ethic is essential to success in any area of life. Working hard matters, whether you are talking about pastoring a church, raising a family, or starting a business. You should work hard. It is not simply a matter of luck that rich people are rich. Thomas Jefferson put it this way: "A mind that is always employed is always happy. . . . I'm a great believer in luck and I find that the harder I work the more I have of it."

But hard work should not be constant drudgery. When we do things God's way, there is plenty of room to experience joy and happiness. The secret is to learn how to work smart, not just hard.

Working Smart

What does it mean to work smart? This is the question we will try to answer in this chapter. In its simplest form, working smart means working with understanding. It is having some of the wisdom of God working in your life and utilizing it in an intelligent manner to do something different than you have done in the past, so that you can get different results than you have in the past.

Understanding begins with the Word of God. It means more than just gaining knowledge of the Bible. You can read all you want, but it will do you no good until you learn to apply the concepts to your everyday life. To gain understanding, according to Proverbs, is to become happy—and that is just the beginning. There are great benefits to wisdom and understanding.

> *Happy is the man who finds wisdom,*
> *And the man who gains understanding.*
> *For her proceeds are better than the profits of silver,*
> *And her gain than fine gold.*

She is more precious than rubies,
And all the things you may desire cannot compare with her.
Length of days is in her right hand,
In her left hand riches and honor.
Her ways are ways of pleasantness,
And all her paths are peace.
She is a tree of life to those who take hold of her.
And happy are all who retain her.
The Lord by wisdom founded the earth;
By understanding He established the heavens;
By His knowledge the depths were broken up,
And clouds drop down the dew. (Prov. 3:13–20)

Wisdom and understanding bring some marvelous things. They include "length of days" and "riches and honor." When we consider that God founded the earth and heavens and essentially controls them by wisdom, understanding, and knowledge, it should become obvious that these three traits are very important for us to consider.

Proverbs speaks often about diligence, but there is usually more to it than the obvious reference to working hard. Take this passage, for example.

He who has a slack hand becomes poor.
But the hand of the diligent makes rich.
He who gathers in summer is a wise son,
But he who sleeps in harvest is a son who causes shame.
Blessings are on the head of the righteous,
But violence covers the mouth of the wicked. (Prov. 10:4–6)

The slack hand in verse four literally means a cupped hand or a closed hand. The diligent person works with an open hand. In other words, the one with a cupped or slack hand is working so as to hold on to things. His hand is closed so as to keep his grip. It is the same idea as the wicked servant who tried to hold on to his mina instead of investing it. He had it, but he never used it.

The hand that becomes rich is the one that is open. He is working eagerly with determination. His diligence is really in the fact that he opens his hand or lets go of things, as the situation requires. He invests. He works smart, not just hard. Diligence, by definition, involves intelligent investment. It is much more than just working hard.

> Diligence, by definition, involves intelligent investment.

Verse five emphasizes that the one who gets rich has understanding of how his business works. He gets the harvest in during the right season. He doesn't try to harvest in the winter when the crops are ruined from sitting in the field, or in the spring when nothing has yet grown. He waits for the right time and then he has the self-discipline to do what needs to be done. He understands his business. This is the person who will hear, "Well done, my good and faithful servant."

The son who sleeps during the harvest brings shame to his father. In the context of this study, that means that the one who just sits on what God has given him and does not multiply it is a disappointment to God. Verse six speaks of blessings on the head of the righteous. "Head" can be translated as "company." Diligence, or working smart with understanding, brings blessing on the company or business of the righteous.

John 10:10, which we examined in an earlier chapter, says, "The thief does not come except to steal and to kill, and to destroy. I have come that they may have life, and that they may have it more abundantly." Most of us can say we have life. We're working. We're usually paying our bills at the end of the month, even if we have to borrow from next month to do it. We've got clothes on our backs, regular meals, and a place to sleep. We have the essentials we need to get by. We have life. But Jesus wants us to have more than that. He wants us to have abundant life—so much that our children's children can't spend it all.

It is this abundance that the devil has tried to steal. He can't kill us. If he could, he would have done it a long time ago. He doesn't like us much. He would have killed Adam and Eve if he could have found a way to do it. He couldn't kill Jesus either. He could tempt Him but he couldn't kill Him. When Jesus died, He gave up his own life. No one took it from Him.

Therefore My Father loves Me, because I lay down My life that I may take it again. No one takes it from Me, but I lay it down of Myself. (John 10:17–18)

The devil has no power to kill. What he can do is deceive. God told Adam and Eve that they could enjoy the fruit of every tree in the garden except one. I believe that tree was the tithe. God reserved it as the only thing to be set aside as His. He gave everything else to them.

The devil overheard the conversation. He realized he couldn't kill them but he could hang around and continuously lie to them until they believed the lie and took the fruit of the one tree God told them not to touch.

It hasn't changed any since then. The devil can't kill you but he can lie to you, and if you believe the lie you open the door for him to come into your life to steal and destroy.

What is the lie? The reason the devil has been able to steal so much from the church is that we have not recognized the lie for what it is. It comes to us in the guise of religion, a perversion of the truth supported by the misapplication of Scripture. The devil has taken Scripture and made religion. And religion is not life. It is always unfruitful.

Jesus began His ministry with power and authority bestowed directly from the Father. At His baptism, the Spirit descended on

Him and the Father spoke the words that expressed how much He was pleased with Jesus (Matt. 3:13–17). But it was not power or authority that Jesus used in the wilderness to overcome temptation. It was an understanding of the Word of God.

The devil came quoting Scripture. He came with religion. But Jesus had more than just a knowledge of the Word. He had understanding and He knew when the devil was misusing it. The second temptation in particular illustrated the devil's methods.

> *Then the devil took Him up into the holy city, set Him on the pinnacle of the temple, and said to Him, "If you are the Son of God, throw Yourself down. For it is written: 'He shall give His angels charge over you,' and 'In their hands they shall bear you up, lest you dash your foot against a stone.'"* (Matt. 4:5–6)

Religion will pull a verse of Scripture out of its context and apply it in a way that takes all of the life out of it and makes it unfruitful. Because Jesus was born in a stable, religion assumed Jesus was poor; yet, they tried to stay at the inn because they could afford it. There was no reason for Jesus to jump. He understood that Psalm 91, the text He used to refute Satan, spoke of God's protection against the attacks of the enemy. It was not a license to do something foolish like jump off a building just to prove a point. In fact, the devil only wanted Jesus to use part of the chapter, since the next verse after the one he quoted had to do with him: "You shall tread upon the lion and the cobra, the young lion and the serpent you shall trample underfoot" (Ps. 91:13).

The Spirit of the Law

Early in his ministry, Jesus began speaking of the difference between the letter of the Law and the spirit of the Law. It produced conflict between Him and the established religious leaders of His day. One of the clearest examples is what came to be known as the Sabbath controversy.

The Pharisees believed healing on the Sabbath was work and thus violated the commandment in Exodus 20:8 to remember the Sabbath to keep it holy. Many such incidents occurred as the religious leaders looked for a reason to arrest Jesus—"And He entered the synagogue again, and a man was there who had a withered hand. So they watched Him closely, whether He would heal him on the Sabbath, so that they might accuse Him" (Mrk. 3:1–2).

The letter of the Law said that Jesus should do whatever the Law said, regardless of the circumstances or the outcome. Jesus had understanding of this commandment. He realized its purpose was to set aside time to focus on God and the Word without the business of life interfering. Every person needs that kind of time during his week. But Jesus also knew that healing those who were sick was not a violation of the principle of the Law. The idea behind the Sabbath was to bring people into experiencing life with God. For someone bound by sickness, healing accomplished the same thing. Healing was a fruit of the relationship Jesus had with His father.

On another occasion Jesus was accused of breaking the Sabbath when His disciples picked the heads of grain as they walked through the fields (Mrk. 2:23–28). The response He made demonstrated the difference between following the Law without understanding and living the principles of the Law through understanding: "The Sabbath was made for man, and not man for the Sabbath" (Mrk. 2:27).

The analogy should be clear. The Pharisees worked very hard at following the Law. Even Jesus acknowledged how hard they worked when He said, "Unless your righteousness exceeds the righteousness of the scribes and Pharisees, you will by no means enter the kingdom of heaven" (Matt. 5:20). But all their work did was wear them out. They weren't working with understanding.

They didn't work smart. Jesus said working smart means gaining understanding of why the Law says what it says so you can learn the principles behind it and apply them to your life. The devil just wants you to work hard. There is freedom and prosperity in having understanding. There is poverty and unfruitfulness in religion and religious attitudes.

> There is freedom and prosperity in having understanding.

Churches have given us some unfruitful and destructive attitudes. First Corinthians 14:34 says, "Let your women keep silent in the churches, for they are not permitted to speak." The devil took that verse and used it to make fifty percent of the body of Christ ineffective for two thousand years. We still deal with it today. A woman recently came up to me and said, "Pastor, I just felt that God instructed me to tell you that your wife should not be up on the platform speaking because women are to be silent in the church."

Paul didn't seem to have a problem with women speaking in the church. Just three chapters earlier, in 1 Corinthians 11, he mentioned women who prayed and prophesied in church, and he didn't tell them to be quiet. His only concern there was that there be order in what occurred. Paul worked closely with Priscilla, who became a pastor along with her husband. The implications are that she was the one who took the leading role, not her husband (Acts 18:18–19; 2 Tim. 4:19; Rom. 16:3). She is always mentioned first, something unusual for that time. Paul speaks of Junia, a woman in the church at Rome, and calls her an apostle (Rom. 16:7). The classic verses in 1 Timothy 2:11–12 that are often used to keep women silent in church are also concerned with disorder and arguing in the church. A quick reading of both letters to Timothy shows that Paul had even more concern about those attitudes among the men than he did with the women. Paul's problem was not with women. It was with disorder.

When you approach these passages of Scripture with understanding, you see that there is order in God's body. Women should not come into the church with the appearance that they are trying to take over the authority of their husbands or stealing their husbands' respect. Religion and religious attitudes just tell women to shut up. The church is finally getting over this foolishness but it is a deception that has caused untold damage.

Another religious notion is that you can pray over your food and then eat anything and it won't hurt you. The truth is that if you eat junk, it is still junk. Praying over it might make it sanctified junk, but it is still junk and it is still bad for you and if you eat enough of it for long enough you will get sick. This misunderstanding of what faith and prayer are all about has caused many Christians to die young.

We all believe we ought to look like Christians. The Bible speaks about dress in several places. First Timothy 2:9 says that women should "adorn themselves in modest apparel, with propriety and moderation, not with braided hair or gold or pearls or costly clothing." The devil takes that Scripture and turns it into a set of rules about how to dress that makes Christians look like a bunch of dysfunctional misfits. We have churches full of people who love Jesus and are good people but they are walking around in little black suits with little pin ties. The women don't wear makeup. They keep their hair in a bun and make sure their dresses are nice and plain and long enough that you can't see their wrists, because we don't want to look at the flesh. They can't wear jewelry of any kind.

All we succeed in doing when we interpret Scripture in this way is to make ourselves look weird. The obvious intent of Paul's writing is not to make people look out of place but to make them look appropriate to the ministry God has called them to. That is just the opposite of looking out of place. It is looking like you belong, that you are capable and competent and that you can be trusted to have some common sense in everything you do. If you just dress funny you will not only have greater difficulty functioning in a normal job but you will have less credibility when you share the Gospel with people around you. That is just what the devil wants.

> God really doesn't want us to look weird. He wants us to look better than everybody else.

It is interesting to go back to the Song of Solomon and see how the bride dressed there. The book contains numerous references to jewelry and clothing that were the best and most attractive available. It would seem that God really doesn't want us to look weird. He wants us to look better than everybody else.

Your cheeks are lovely with ornaments.
Your neck with chains of gold.
We will make you ornaments of gold
With studs of silver. (Song 1:10–11)

You have ravished my heart
With one look of your eyes,
With one link of your necklace. (Song 4:9)

How much better than wine is your love,
And the scent of your perfumes
Than all spices! (Song 4:10)

And the fragrance of your garments
Is like the fragrance of Lebanon. (Song 4:11)

Your head crowns you like Mount Carmel,
And the hair of your head is like purple;
A king is held captive by your tresses. (Song 7:5)

The devil has used religion to keep us uneducated. We want our children to go to Bible school so they don't have to experience the pressures of the world. We want them to be spiritual. Yet when they get out, all they know is some information about the Bible. They don't know how to get a job or how to keep a job when they get it. They don't have any understanding of how to relate to the rest of the world.

In the World, Not of the World

The sad part of all of this is that because many Christians can't relate to the world, they have no understanding of how to share Jesus with the world either. They think that being bold for Jesus means saying and doing weird things. They walk down the aisle in the grocery store and suddenly shout, "Praise God. I found the bread. Thank you, Jesus." People are not impressed with weirdness or ignorance or how loud you can be. But when they see the life of Jesus manifested in a person who is successful, they take notice. They need to know Jesus is interested in making His people successful in everyday life. Jesus is not interested in making them weird. He wants them to stand out because they are successful, not because they are strange.

The devil quotes Scripture that says we are to be separate from the world. Revelation says, "Come out of her, my people, lest you share in her sins, and lest you receive of her plagues" (Rev. 18:4). As a result Christians have fled from politics, from the entertainment industry, and from the arts. Then they complain because so many ungodly things happen in all of those areas. But why should they expect anything different?

When the Bible says we are not to be of this world, it means we should not participate in the world's way of thinking. It does not mean we go hide somewhere in the back of the church so we can be spiritual. God expects us to take an active part in changing the world around us. We can't do that unless we get involved. Christians should be filling the Congress, the state legislatures, the city councils, and the school boards of America. Most of us don't even know when the school board meets. We're not involved. We're not aware. And we're not effective.

The devil has used religion to make an issue of church doctrine. I hate church doctrine. I don't preach church doctrine. I believe the Bible. Doctrine is too often the result of twisting the principles of the Word of God. Probably seventy percent of the Christians in America today have been robbed of blessing, health, and prosperity because of church doctrine. They are the ones who believe God makes them sick to teach them lessons and that He makes them poor to keep them humble.

In all of these areas, the devil has stolen from us the best that God wanted us to have. It is religion that says money is evil and that the rich can't get to heaven. When we have understanding of the Word, then we realize we can't do the things God wants His church to do unless we have money. Understanding is extremely important in the plans God has for us. We can't get anywhere without it.

The church is finally coming out of this deception. The whole world belongs to Jesus and, since we are joint heirs with Him, it belongs to us. God wants us to enjoy it and He wants us to use it to accomplish His purposes. With a right understanding of this we begin to see that working smart, not just hard, is God's perfect will for His people.

Working smart means realizing that it all belongs to God anyway. We saw earlier how Joseph ended up owning all the land and cattle of Egypt. He offered seed back to the people for the price of one-fifth of their produce.

Then Joseph said to the people, "Indeed I have bought you and your land this day for Pharaoh. Look, here is seed for you, and you shall sow the land. And it shall come to pass in the harvest that

you shall give one-fifth to Pharaoh. Four-fifths shall be your own,
as seed for the field and for your food, for those of your households
and as food for your little ones." (Gen. 47:23–24)

Joseph is a picture of the New Testament Jesus. He owns everything but gives back the seed so we can plant it and cause it to multiply. In return he asks that we give the tithe and the offering. Like the people of Egypt we can say, "You have saved our lives" (Gen. 47:25).

I hope by now you understand the importance of the tithe. But that is one-tenth. Joseph asked for one-fifth. Does that mean you should be giving twenty percent or ten? In Malachi, God refers to both tithes and offerings.

Will a man rob God?
Yet you have robbed Me!
But you say,
"In what way have we robbed You?"
In tithes and offerings. (Mal. 3:8)

When He says to bring the whole tithe, He is referring to the offering as well. The word "whole" means the complete offering. God says He will open the windows of heaven and pour out a blessing so great that it cannot be contained. The picture given in the original Hebrew implies that the tithe opens the windows of heaven and it also causes God to rebuke the devourer, but the offering causes the rain to come forth that waters the seed and makes it multiply.

This does not mean you have to give exactly twenty percent. You should purpose in your heart what you will give over and above your tithe. This is the truth of giving. The devil doesn't want you to tithe at all so he has taken Scripture and used it to deceive us. He points to Corinthians: "So let each one give as he purposes in his heart" (2 Cor. 9:7). He says that the Scripture allows you to give any amount you want. As a result of this verse, the church is inundated every Christmas and Easter with one dollar bills because that is how much people purpose to give. They point to the Bible and say, "It says here I should give what I feel like giving, and I feel like giving a dollar."

When you have understanding of the Scripture, not just knowledge, you will see that Paul was not talking about the tithe. He was referring to an offering being taken to the church in Jerusalem for their assistance. It was essentially a missions gift (2 Cor. 9:1–5). The tithe protected their possessions. The rest of the offering brought blessing. Religion ignores the context, which emphasizes that you have to invest in order to multiply.

> *But this I say; He who sows sparingly will also reap sparingly, and he who sows bountifully will also reap bountifully. So let each one give as he purposes in his heart, not grudgingly or of necessity; for God loves a cheerful giver.* (2 Cor. 9:6–7)

So, you can give what you feel like giving but if you don't tithe ten percent, the devil will steal what you have. If you give a small offering beyond your tithe, you can expect small results. The point of all this is that the devil says that working hard means putting your head down and plodding on, putting in long days and never having any fun. He will quote Scripture to support this deception. But when you have understanding you see that working hard in the biblical sense includes working smart, becoming financially literate, and enjoying the blessings of God as you use them for the building of His kingdom.

In closing this chapter I will leave you with a few thoughts about how to make your money work for you from *The Richest Man in Babylon* by George S. Clason. I include them in King James English, in case you still feel the need for a religious appearance.

Five Ways to Make Your Money Work for You

1. Start thy purse to fattening. In other words, for every ten coins you put in, take no more than nine out. In a short time you will have plenty of money to invest.
2. Control thine expenditures. Expenses will always grow to equal your income unless you take control.
3. Make thy "gold" multiply. Put every coin possible into laboring that it may reproduce after its own kind—even as the flock of the field—and a stream of wealth will flow constantly into your purse.

> Study investments wisely before parting with hard-earned money.

4. Guard thy treasure for loss. The tithe protects your stuff. Offerings are seeds that can produce and multiply. Also study to know what you are investing in. Study investments wisely before parting with hard-earned money.
5. Make thy dwelling a profitable investment. Pay it off early and let it make you money. Build assets, not liabilities.

Chapter 8 Summary

What, Me Work?

A good work ethic is essential to success in any area of life, but if all you do is work, it will become drudgery. Learn to work smart and there will be plenty of room to experience joy and happiness.

Working smart means working with understanding. It means working in an intelligent manner to do something different than you have done in the past, so that you can get different results.

If you always do what you've always done, you'll always get what you always got.

How to Work Smart

Proverbs 10:4–6 indicates what it means to work smart: "A slack hand becomes poor, but the hand of the diligent makes rich."

1. A slack hand is really one who holds on to things. He won't invest. Diligence, by definition, involves intelligent investment.
2. The one who gets rich understands how business works. He does business in a manner that is effective.

The Spirit of the Law and the Letter of the Law

Religious people work very hard at following the letter of the Law, but all they do is wear themselves out. Following the spirit of the Law means enjoying the benefits that come from understanding the principles of the Law and applying them to your life.

Because of religious thinking, the devil has stolen from us the best that God wanted us to have. Religious thinking has made us believe that money is evil and the rich can't get into heaven.

When we have understanding, we know that we can't do the things that God wants us to do without money. We will then learn to work smarter, not just harder.

Don't knock the rich. When did a poor person give you a job?

Small Start, Big Finish

THERE IS AN OLD MATHEMATICAL CALCULATION THAT ILLUSTRATES how much a small investment can grow. If you agreed to work for someone for exactly one month, just thirty days, and you worked the first day for one cent, doubling your salary every day for the month, you might feel that you weren't making very much. The second day you would get two cents. The third day it would increase to four cents. By the twelfth day you would still only be making $20.48.

But things would increase rapidly after that. On the fifteenth day, halfway through the month, you would receive $163.84. It would go over a thousand dollars on the eighteenth day and by the last day of the month your pay would be more than five million dollars. When you add up all of the daily amounts it totals $10,737,418.23. Not bad for starting with just a penny!

This tremendous increase results from multiplication. If the only thing we are looking for in life is a good raise or a better paying job, then we are adding, not multiplying. Using the same starting pay of one penny a day and adding a penny to it each day for a month you can see the difference. You will receive one cent the first day, two cents the second day, three cents the third day and so on. By the end of the month you will have $4.65, a far cry from ten million. Even if you started with a dollar instead of a penny you still would only have $465. But this is the way we are thinking when we consider getting a raise to be wealth. We are adding when God wants us to multiply.

There are many scenarios that involve starting small and developing it into great wealth. If you have a child who is sixteen years old or younger, you could begin investing $50 each month into an IRA until he is able to cover the monthly payment. Assuming an interest rate of 12.5 percent, if he continues to put the same monthly amount in consistently until he is sixty-five the IRA will have approximately 1.7 million dollars in it. That is a lot of money for such a small start.

The earlier you start, the better you will be. If a nineteen-year-old takes $2,000 a year for eight years and invests it in a mutual fund that pays 12 percent interest, you would have a total investment of $16,000. By the time that person is sixty-five years old there will be 1.6 million dollars in the account.

If you waited until you were twenty-seven to begin and invested $2,000 a year until you were sixty-five, you would have a total of $74,000 but you will only end up with a total of $800,000 in the account. Starting early is important but even if you are older than that now, you still need to start. It doesn't take much to begin.

A parent who takes $1,000 on the day his baby is born and opens an account at 12 percent interest will have $40,000 in college funds by the time the child grows to the age of eighteen. If the child leaves it alone until he is sixty-five it will be well over a million dollars.

Everyone begins small. It is as biblical as anything we have talked about so far. Scripture abounds with examples of successful people who began with very limited resources and accomplished great things through intelligent and disciplined investment. God loves to see the multiplication. "For who has despised the day of small things?" (Zech. 4:10). Job certainly experienced great loss. He had virtually nothing left but he still knew how to start small and end up big—"Though your beginning was small, yet your latter end would increase abundantly" (Job 8:7).

Even Jesus had to start small. The son of God had to begin as a baby and grow. He had to study and learn. Luke tells us that He "increased in wisdom and stature, and in favor with God and men" (Luk. 2:52). Jesus studied until He was thirty. Then He began His ministry small. He showed up at the Jordan River to be baptized by John the Baptist. He came alone. There was no marketing department to launch Him on His way, no press releases to alert the media that He was beginning to preach, no photographers to capture the moment for future documentaries. He wasn't popular then. It was just Him and John.

From there He was led into the wilderness to be tempted by the devil. It was one of the most important moments in His life but there was no crowd to see it and no one to help, just Jesus and the devil.

Jesus began teaching for a while before He called His disciples. He did not have a big organization behind Him, just Himself and His calling to preach. Then He began calling disciples. There were only twelve to begin with but as He trained them, the twelve turned into seventy-two and by the time He left the earth

> Jesus started small but He built on what He had and multiplied it.

there were 120 gathered in the upper room who very quickly became 3,000 and then 5,000. Jesus started small but He built on what He had and multiplied it.

It is important to realize that the success Jesus had was more than just being a good Bible teacher. He was successful in every way. He looked successful and He acted successful. He dressed as a successful person. His clothing was so valuable that even at His crucifixion the Roman soldiers would not cut it up. They gambled for it instead so as not to destroy it. If some homeless guy walked up to you and said, "Follow me," you would laugh at best, or more likely sneer a little. You would not follow someone who gave every indication to you of being a complete loser. People followed Jesus because He looked and acted like He knew where He was going. He started small but He knew His purpose and pursued it with confidence and power. He multiplied what He had and it got the attention of everyone in the country.

> You would not follow someone who gave every indication to you of being a complete loser.

Luke 19 describes an incident in the ministry of Jesus that illustrates the kind of appeal He had. He passed through Jericho on His way to Jerusalem. He was at the peak of His ministry. When He got to Jerusalem, He was met with a huge crowd that placed palm branches in front of Him and shouted praises to Him. The events that would take place there after the triumphal entry into the city gates would provide salvation for all men and would establish His church.

The Tax Collector

In the Old Testament, Jericho was the first city God gave to Joshua as he brought Israel into the Promised Land. It was also the only city from which God told them not to take any spoils for themselves. Everything there belonged to God. The city of Jericho represented the tithe, the first fruits of the new land. Jesus stopped there on His way to Jerusalem.

There was a man in Jericho named Zacchaeus (Luk. 19:2). From Luke we know that he was a chief tax collector; he was also rich. It is important to understand clearly the details of this picture. We heard the story of Zacchaeus in Sunday school. We really only remember two things about him. He was a tax collector and he was short. We never think much about it past that. We understand he was a sinner and that Jesus went to his house, but we tend to overlook some important points.

Zacchaeus was not only a tax collector but a "chief" tax collector, which means he was in charge. He was possibly the head of the whole region. He undoubtedly made a good salary. He was also rich, and didn't become rich just on a salary. He was a man who understood investments. In chapter 6 we discussed the government issued bonds that the Roman Empire used. Zacchaeus was probably one of the people who collected taxes to pay off those bonds. He understood the system from being intimately involved in it. He knew how investments worked. He was not just a chief tax collector. He was very wealthy.

The next thing to notice about Zacchaeus is that he wanted to see Jesus (Luk. 19:3). He went to a lot of trouble to see Him. Zacchaeus was short and the crowd was tall. So he climbed a tree along the path Jesus was walking on so he could see over the crowd.

As I already said, you would not follow a homeless person. You would want to follow someone who is successful. The rich do not come out to see the poor come to town. In fact, the poor don't turn out to see the poor. They come out to see the rich. And the rich come out to see the richer. The size of the crowd was an indication of how successful Jesus had become during the three years since His ministry started with nothing but Himself.

We know that Zacchaeus was rich so it is safe to say that Jesus was even more successful than him. His desire was to see someone even more successful than Himself. Jesus hung out with people who were going somewhere. He went to parties at the homes of the wealthiest people in town. When He called His disciples, He spoke only to men who were successful, working businessmen. Mary Magdalene and the other women who contributed financially to the support of Jesus and His disciples were wealthy.

Jesus was accused of hanging out with sinners, but it should be noted that the ones making those accusations were the religious people of the day. Even today those who are religious and who don't have money accuse those who do have money of being sinners. To a religious mind, the possession of wealth could not possibly be spiritual. Of course the kind of sinners that Jesus was accused of associating with were rich ones. Gluttons were the ones who could afford to eat a lot, and drunkards were the ones who could afford to drink a lot, but those rich people were who Jesus spent His time with.

He ministered to everyone, both rich and poor. When He went into a city the Word tells us that they were all healed. His love and compassion did not take note of how well a person dressed or how successful they looked, but the people He hung out with were rich. They were the members of the community who, because of their wealth, could have the greatest influence on the world around them. They were the ones best prepared to build His kingdom. It is significant that out of all the crowd in Jericho that day, Jesus pushed to the back of the line and found Zacchaeus in the tree. He gave such special attention to him that He not only talked to him but interrupted His trip to Jerusalem in order to go to Zacchaeus's house. Zacchaeus was an influential man in a position to do a great deal of good. He received Jesus joyfully (Luk. 19:6). But the crowd complained. "But when they saw it, they all complained, saying, 'He has gone to be a guest with a man who is a sinner'" (Luk. 19:7). Zacchaeus was a tax collector, so there is some question immediately about how honest he was, but the Bible doesn't actually say he was particularly dishonest. His response to Jesus was certainly not the words of an irresponsible man—"Look, Lord, I give half of my goods to the poor; and if I have taken anything from anyone by false accusation, I restore fourfold" (Luk. 19:8).

Zacchaeus was ready to clean up any wrong things he had done. With the wealth that he had, he was in a position to accomplish much for the furthering of the Gospel. It appears that Jesus was less concerned with His own reputation than He was with ministry to this influential man in the city of Jericho. He saw Zacchaeus's willingness to use his wealth to help the community and He declared that salvation had come to that house. Salvation had come to reconcile the creation.

Today salvation has come to this house, because he also is a son of Abraham; for the Son of Man has come to seek and to save that which was lost. (Luk. 19:9–10)

The phrase "son of Abraham" could be interpreted in several ways. The most obvious is that Zacchaeus was a descendant of Abraham or, in other words, he was Jewish. Abraham was the "father of Israel."

Take note of the fact, however, that in the New Testament, Abraham is connected to the people of faith. It says in Genesis 15:6 that because he believed God, it was accounted to him as righteousness. God promised to make him a father of many nations, not just of Israel (Gen. 17:5). He became the father of all who have faith.

Therefore it is of faith that it might be according to grace, so that the promise might be sure to all the seed, not only to those who are of the law, but also to those who are of the faith of Abraham, who is the father of us all. (Rom. 4:16)

When Zacchaeus began giving away his wealth, he demonstrated an attitude of faith. That, more than his Jewish ancestry, made him a son of Abraham. It was also what prompted Jesus to say that salvation had come to his house.

There are two aspects of salvation that must be considered.

First is the spiritual application of being born again. When you accept Jesus as your Savior, that is, when you believe that He died for your sin, and you ask Him to become the Lord of your life, you are saved. You receive new life and you are free from the penalty of sin, which is death. That is certainly a part of what Jesus meant when He said to Zacchaeus that salvation had come to him.

But the word "salvation" comes from the Hebrew word yasha. The name "Jesus" comes from the same root and means salvation. The Hebrew meaning has a picture of coming from a narrow confined place into a wide open space where there is abundance, freedom, riches, and opulence. When salvation came to Zacchaeus, it not only meant new spiritual life, but it also brought great wealth, joy, and prosperity.

With this definition in mind, look at the last thing Jesus said to Zacchaeus. "The Son of Man has come to seek and to save that which was lost." He did not say "those" who were lost. He said "that" which was lost. "Those" would mean people. "That" means things. I don't need to say that God wants to save people. We know that. But we need to see that He wants to save things as well. He wants to save the earth. Jesus came to restore this earth to the fullness and the wealth that He originally wanted for His people. Salvation includes saving your finances and your prosperity.

The process of sowing seed and cultivating it as it multiplies is as old as the earth and will continue for as long as the earth does. The process of investment and multiplication follows the same pattern.

While the earth remains,
Seedtime and harvest,
Cold and heat,
Winter and summer,
And day and night
Shall not cease. (Gen. 8:22)

God never intended for this pattern to change. From the beginning of time, He gave seed to the sower. The first fruit or the tithe from the harvest was to go back to God. The first fruit was always the strongest seed. The second fruit was the second strongest seed. It was intended for investment. The rest was for the enjoyment of the one who harvested it. If you eat the second fruit you have nothing left to invest.

The seed that is necessary for investment, the seed that will make you wealthy, does not have to be very big. It does not take a whole lot for God to multiply your investment and make you wealthy, but it does require that you do something. All too often we think that God is just going to throw money at us because we tithed a couple of times. God will bless the work of our hands but our hands have to work first. We have to become financially literate so that we can handle the wealth when it comes. Most of us would like to start very big, but the truth is we are probably not ready for it. God wants us to learn how to manage wealth. When we are faithful in little things, He entrusts us with greater things. For some, the most important part of becoming wealthy will be the first step, which might be as small as learning how to balance their checkbooks.

We noted earlier in the chapter that Jesus started small. He wasn't just born and then crucified for mankind. Rather He grew and developed the character to accomplish His call. He gained experience. He learned to understand people, life, and death.

There are no shortcuts to great wealth. When you try to find easy money, you rob yourself of many of the lessons that you need for success. You must learn discipline, passion, generosity, and creativity. You must develop the character of a millionaire. The world determines wealth and success by what you have. God determines wealth and success by what you give. Success is not

> You must develop the character of a millionaire.

about what you get but what you become. You must be careful as you develop the characteristics of a millionaire that you own your possessions. If you do not maintain the right attitude, your possessions will begin to own you.

Above all remember that you must begin small and grow. Jesus did and before He was finished, He was ministering to the most wealthy and influential people in the country. To have a big finish you need a small start on a strong foundation. Don't try to rush it.

Chapter 9 Summary

Small Start, Big Finish

Most people think of increase as getting a raise. To have true wealth, however, we must make our money multiply instead of just adding to it.

The Principle of Multiplication

With the principle of multiplication, you don't need much to get started. If you work thirty days, agreeing to be paid one cent the first day and doubling your pay every day after that, by the end of a month you will have over ten million dollars.

Jesus started small, a ministry that was just Himself. By the time He finished, His ministry had multiplied to twelve disciples, then seventy-two, then to thousands.

Reconcile the Earth

Jesus' ministry reached the point where He influenced not only the poor, but also the wealthiest and most influential.

Zacchaeus was very wealthy (Luk. 19). He wanted to see Jesus, which indicates that Jesus was even more successful than him. Jesus understood the impact of wealth.

Zacchaeus wanted to clean up the wrongs that he had done in his life. When he started giving money away, it was a declaration of faith.

The change in Zacchaeus prompted Jesus to say that salvation had come to that house. He also stated that He had come to save that which was lost—not just people, but the earth as well. He came to reconcile every part of the earth to His kingdom. That included finances.

By starting small and planting a seed, an investment, we begin the process of bringing salvation to our finances. We also reconcile the earth to the kingdom of God by bringing the wealth of the world into God's purposes.

10

Bulldog Tenacity

THERE IS A STORY ABOUT A BLIMP IN THE STATE OF NEW YORK THAT was preparing for a flight. The basket was being loaded with all of the passengers. The blimp was anchored by a rope held by about seventy people. Suddenly a gust of wind blew through the area and the blimp was carried into the air unexpectedly. Most of the people on the rope let go, but a few were so taken by surprise that they hung on and were carried into the air. By the time they let go, they were already a few hundred feet in the air. Sixteen of them died.

But there was one man who didn't let go. He knew that if he did, he would die, so he wrapped his leg around the rope and clung to it. He later said he knew the blimp would have to come down eventually. When everyone else fell off, he was able to tie the rope around his waist and ride it out until the blimp touched down again. He had a bulldog tenacity that saved his life.

When you look at a bulldog, the first thing you notice is the strange shape of his face. His teeth are clear out to the front of his head while his nose is way back from the front of his face. It is this unusual design of a bulldog's head that makes him distinctive from other dogs.

There is a reason for this design. When a bulldog bites your leg, he will not let go. Most dogs bite and hang on for a minute, but they have to let go because they can't breathe. A bulldog doesn't have that problem since his nose is so far back from his teeth. He doesn't have to let go until he chooses to.

We have looked at many of the attitudes that are necessary for gaining wealth. They are not complicated but they are essential. You need to have confidence, passion, discipline, ambition, creativity. These are all characteristics that are available to any person who will take the time to study business and learn how it works. Once you have these characteristics, however, you then need tenacity. Don't give up until you get it right. Learn from your mistakes and try again. Peter Daniels, one of the wealthiest men in Australia, started six businesses before he finally succeeded. But he didn't quit.

When we walk in the Spirit, we will manifest the fruit of the Spirit—"But the fruit of the Spirit is love, joy, peace, longsuffering, kindness, goodness, faithfulness, gentleness, self-control. Against such there is no law" (Gal. 5:22–23). Longsuffering is another word for perseverance. The person who walks in God's perfect will is not a quitter. He has persevered, he has overcome. Regardless of your background, your history or your circumstances, God has given you everything you need to become wealthy, if you will just do it His way and not give up. Too many people have a wishbone where they should have a backbone. We need to heed the advice of Hebrews.

> Too many people have a wishbone where they should have a backbone.

And we desire that each one of you show the same diligence to the full assurance of hope until the end, that you do not become slug-

gish, but imitate those who through faith and patience inherit the promises. (Heb. 6:11–12)

Building wealth takes time. It is a process that you have to work through to develop the skills you need to have money. There is a beautiful valley over the hill but you have to climb the hill to get to it. If you follow these four steps, you will become wealthy.

1. Plan purposefully.
2. Prepare prayerfully.
3. Proceed positively.
4. Pursue persistently.

The Baby Boomers

We are living at a moment in history that is unparalleled for its potential to investors. We are on the edge of the greatest affluence America has ever known. Since the early 1990s, we have had a continual financial growth pattern that will continue for at least two or three decades.

The reason I can be so confident about this is that I have seen the trends of the baby boomer generation. These are the people born between 1946 and 1964. They are seventy million strong and they control three quarters of the wealth in America today. They are unique in American history for their approach to life and the way they deal with money.

Most baby boomers were teenagers in the sixties. They were raised with a free mentality, the hippie generation of free love and doing whatever feels good. They have grown up and left behind flower power and tie-dyed clothes, but something of that approach to life has carried over. And now they have some money.

Since 1990, the rich have gotten richer, but so have the poor. Our standard of living has improved. The power of the dollar has increased. Property values have gone up. The average American is better off than ever before. The baby boomers have become affluent.

And they are spending their money. They don't care about saving it. When they want things, they go and get them. That's the way they have always thought and it is still how they think. They have a degree of self-centeredness that has some negative aspects,

> The "If it feels good, do it" mentality is still alive and well.

but this same trait also fuels our economy. The "If it feels good, do it" mentality is still alive and well. Education levels are dropping because people don't want to go to the trouble of learning. The ability to communicate or write is declining rapidly. Relationships are becoming less important to more people. We have a generation coming up that has no boundaries. They are creative but they will attack one another at the drop of a hat. This has made society more lawless and less logical.

But this attitude also means that they are spending money as never before in history. If they want it, they buy it. It doesn't matter what the interest rates are. It doesn't even matter if they can afford it. They will buy it.

There is a struggle going on between the baby boomers and the Federal Reserve Bank. The rich don't want the poor to continue to prosper. By manipulating interest rates and raising oil prices they hope to continue to get richer and keep the poor poor. The baby boomers aren't cooperating, however. Our parents saved money and still had nothing. The baby boomers don't save at all. They spend. The stock market drops and they spend anyway. Oil prices go up and the baby boomers drive their luxury cars anyway, and those vehicles aren't four-cylinder models either. They cling to their eight-cylinder gas hogs because they want the gas hogs. The government raises interest rates and the baby boomers buy a house anyway.

Yet as this group grows older, they will need more medical attention and they will demand it at lower prices. Inflation will drop. Medical expenses will drop. People with the attitude that the baby boomers have will not stop spending for very long, no matter what is happening around them.

The economy is emotionally driven. Baby boomers say that they are buying only what they need, but the truth is that they buy what they want and, with the use of credit, they buy it when they want it. This trend will not end until the baby boomers stop spending, and that won't happen until at least 2010 or 2015. For those who are prepared for this economic climate, the opportunity for investment is enormous. Knowing that the economy is emotionally driven, you can begin using your emotions for your benefit instead of letting them work against you.

Emotion is really energy in motion. The poor are driven by the emotions of fear and greed. The rich are driven by passion and faith. The poor are driven by the fear of not having money so they work hard to have it. But when they have it, the greed for other things and the fear of not having them drives them to buy liabilities, which keeps them poor. Your desire for wealth does not have to be bad, however. It can be the emotion that drives you to get control of your finances and become financially literate. The best emotions are those that are tied to the fruit of the Spirit— love, joy, peace, longsuffering, kindness, goodness, faithfulness, gentleness, and self-control. If you develop these emotions, they will drive you to wealth that enables you to build the kingdom of God. If you develop the emotions of the flesh, they will drive you to poverty.

Knowing these things, we can begin to get some general ideas about where to invest. The wants and needs of the baby boomers will drive the marketplace. As we understand them, we can make intelligent decisions. Creativity in investment is a good thing. Never begin thinking that it's all been done. In 1929, the man in charge of the United States Patent Office made the statement that everything that can be invented has already been invented. He is now remembered exclusively for being stupid.

Pharmaceuticals are good investments as long as the company is keeping pace with new developments. Do not invest in any company that does not have research and development going on. They will quickly become obsolete if they are not creating new products that keep up with the market. Any company that tries to live on what it did yesterday will go broke.

Pharmaceutical companies that are moving forward, talking about life extension and improving health, are creating products baby boomers will buy. They want to live forever and they will spend their money to try to do it. This is the emotion of the time.

Tech stocks are good but they can be very volatile. The industry is going through such rapid transition that many opportunities are available. But the risk is greater also. The development of super microchips will radically alter the tech stocks. Computers will become so small that they will easily fit in your pocket. The Internet is really in its infant stage. Tremendous strides will be made there over the next ten years.

The entertainment industry—television, movies, and recording—are already being impacted by the Internet. You can pull music off of your computer and burn your own CDs at home.

Convenience and quality are the things that sell. That is what motivates the baby boomers. When investing, look for companies that have premium quality. They customize their products to the desires of the baby boomers. They have fast response and delivery times and they emphasize personal service.

> Convenience and quality are the things that sell.

Toyota developed a spin-off company that catered to the baby boomers. It is called Lexus. The Lexus is a car designed specifically for this group's tastes. It does everything but drive itself. It has the best of any feature that you can put in a car. The service is personalized, everything a baby boomer could want . . . and they don't care if it costs $60,000.

Stock was sixty cents a share when the company first started. It increased by seven times in the first year. Today it has gone up over one hundred and fifty times. It sells because baby boomers want the best.

That is the reason why we bought from foreign producers when American products were inferior in quality. We didn't care where the things came from as long as they were good.

Companies such as UPS and FedEx have been successful because they have figured out ways to personalize their service. If you want it there tomorrow, they will get it there tomorrow.

If you keep these trends in mind as you invest, it will help you to determine which companies are on the right track to be successful. This is all part of being financially literate. If you want to make money in the stock market, you have to know how the stock market works. Here are a few basic principles that you can utilize as you prepare for investment.

Stock prices rise and fall irregularly but over time they persistently go up. The value of the businesses behind the stocks tends to increase over time as the earnings are directed back into the businesses. If you invest in the stock of stable companies that meet the criteria we have discussed and just leave it alone over a long period of time, it will almost always increase in value. There is always some risk but the history of the stock market shows that it has consistently gone up.

Long term bonds are extremely good investments as long as they are compound. They are relatively safe investments. In order to be most successful, the individual investor needs to invest, not speculate. Study the companies and accounts in which you are investing. Know their history. Have a good idea of what the potential return is before you put money in. You won't eliminate risk but you can minimize it. Always have a rule of thumb in mind for the appropriate time to sell. Always have at least a minimum of your investments in stocks.

As a general rule, when you buy stock, sixty percent of your investment should be in stock and forty percent should be in bonds. When stock goes down, bonds go up. When stock goes up, bonds go down. Once you are locked into a bond program, it can't go down, but this general rule will help you know how and when to buy.

Wealth in the Kingdom of God

This kind of information is often nothing more than common sense when you understand how money works. For most Christians, however, it is completely foreign. The church has lived for so long with wrong perceptions of what the Bible says about money that we can't even comprehend the simplest elements of investment. We have been programmed with "poor." We read the Bible through "poor" perceptions. Poverty has been the result.

Jesus came to the earth to save everyone, rich and poor. But it seems that evangelical Christians don't feel right if they preach to the rich. It is fascinating to me as I speak to pastors around the world how much this perspective has limited the scope of their ministries and created problems for church growth. Many have called and asked my advice. Their churches are struggling financially. There just isn't enough money coming in to pay the bills and keep the church operating.

My first question is, "What are you doing with your ministry?"

"Well, we are feeding the hungry and helping the poor. We are taking teams into the projects and preaching to the lost there."

I ask, "Is that your whole focus? How do you advertise? Who do you market to? How are you reaching people?"

The problem seems to be that they are preaching to the poor, who get saved and come into the church and stay poor, so that the church stays poor. When the church is poor, it is impossible to finance the programs that the church needs to have to continue the ministry. The money that makes a church run doesn't drop out of the sky. It comes from the people in the church, and if none of them have any money, then the church isn't going to do much. It can't afford to. We have allowed religion to cloud our perceptions of what Scripture says. For example, James makes a reference to showing partiality.

> When the church is poor, it is impossible to finance the programs that the church needs to have to continue the ministry.

For if there should come into your assembly a man with gold rings, in fine apparel, and there should also come in a poor man in filthy clothes, and you pay attention to the one wearing the fine clothes and say to him, "You sit here in a good place," and say to the poor man, "You stand there," or, "Sit here at my footstool," have you not shown partiality among yourselves, and become judges with evil thoughts? (James 2:2–4)

Religion has caused us to give an inordinate amount of attention to the poor and to ignore the rich. But that is as much partiality as ignoring the poor. Jesus came to minister to both. We saw in the last chapter that He hung out with some very wealthy people. He ministered to people like Bartemaus, who was poor and blind, but He also ministered to the centurion and to Jairus who was a ruler in the synagogue. He ministered to the woman who had an issue of blood. She was wealthy enough to be able to pay many doctors for many years before she came to Jesus. Jesus did not show partiality to the poor any more than He did to the rich. The rich were necessary to finance the ministry.

If you decided to run for president of the United States, you would not expect to win without spending some money. You would have to pay for postage, television time, advertising on the radio. You would have to travel from city to city with a large crew of people, buy them food, and pay for their transportation. There would be fliers and bulletins and flags and buttons and bumper stickers. You might think that you could do a lot of good for the country if you could get elected but if you don't have any money, you won't make it.

The ministry is no different. If the church has no money, it won't have a ministry either. And if no one in the church has money, then the church won't have money. Jesus knew all of this and He surrounded Himself with people who could finance the ministry He was engaged in. It is interesting that most of the people who were touched by Jesus and wanted to follow Him were told to go home. The man in the country of the Gadarenes who was delivered from a legion of demons wanted to follow Him. In fact the Bible says that he begged Jesus to let him go (Mrk. 5:18). But Jesus basically said, "You are a mess. Go home and straighten your life out. You're not ready to follow Me on the road."

Those people who Jesus called to follow Him were people who were working or wealthy. The disciples all had jobs. With our misconceptions about ministering to the poor, we would have gone to the unemployment line to look for disciples. Give them a job and teach them how to be ministers and they will be fine. But Jesus called businessmen. Peter owned a fishing business and it was able to operate for three years while he was away on the road. We know that because he went back to it after the crucifixion. Levi was a tax collector. We saw how well Zacchaeus did in the same occupation. The women who followed Jesus were wealthy enough that Luke says: "These women provided for Him from their substance" (Luk. 8:3). They included Mary Magdalene and Joanna, who was the wife of Cuza, the manager of Herod's household. Jesus took some wealthy people on the road with Him. The poor He sent home to put their lives in order.

Jesus could attract the rich to Him primarily because He was wealthy Himself. Even if you assume that Joseph and Mary were poor at the time Jesus was born, by the time the magi left, they had plenty of gold, frankincense, and myrrh. These were gifts of great value, fit for a king. They set Jesus and His parents up so well that they could easily travel for several years. They relocated to Egypt, back to Judea, then to Nazareth, without having to worry about how to pay for it. If they were poor, they didn't stay that way for long.

The Eye of the Needle

A popular verse that people use to try and say that Jesus was poor is in Matthew—"Foxes have holes and birds of the air have nests, but the Son of Man has nowhere to lay His head" (Matt. 8:20). The context of the verse is a reply to a scribe who wanted to follow Jesus. All He was saying with this expression was, "My trip is too long and you wouldn't be able to do it."

Another verse often quoted to prove that Jesus was poor concerns a camel.

> *Assuredly, I say to you that it is hard for a rich man to enter the*
> *kingdom of heaven. And again I say to you, it is easier for a camel*
> *to go through the eye of a needle than for a rich man to enter the*
> *kingdom of God.* (Matt. 19:23–24)

To begin with, this comment followed an incident in which Jesus was approached by a rich young man who wanted to follow Him. The man asked what he should do to have eternal life. Jesus told him to keep the commandments. He asked which ones and Jesus listed several. The young man said, "All these things I have kept from my youth. What do I still lack?" (Matt. 19:20). Jesus responded by identifying the biggest problem the young man had. "If you want to be perfect, go, sell what you have and give to the poor, and you will have treasure in heaven; and come, follow Me" (Matt. 19:21).

The problem wasn't that the young man was rich. It was that he was depending on his wealth rather than on God. The money owned him, not the other way around. "But when the young man heard that saying, he went away sorrowful, for he had great possessions" (Matt. 19:22).

The comments Jesus made about the camel were in response to this young man. The eye of the needle was a rock formation that had a small passage through it. A camel could fit—but just barely. It became a game to try and get the camel to pass through. The only way it could be done was to blindfold the camel so that it wouldn't be distracted and frightened by the tightness of the opening.

Jesus was not saying that the rich could not enter the kingdom. He was explaining that those who are rich might need to be blindfolded so they cannot see their circumstances. If they look at their wealth, then they tend to depend on it, not on God. Depending on your money won't get you into the kingdom, but when you depend on God, your wealth is a great asset to the kingdom.

A careful study of the life of Jesus shows many times when He said and did things that would never be possible if He wasn't wealthy. We have missed so much of what is said because we started out with the wrong perceptions. These perceptions have to change for you to gain the wealth that God wants you to have. It is easy to fail. Anyone can do it. It is not that hard to succeed, but you have to have perseverance. Failure is defined as the path of least persistence.

Abraham Lincoln is a lasting example of persistence. He was born in a one-room log cabin in a rural area. He grew up in a poor family. His brother died in infancy. His sister died while giving birth. His mother died when he was nine. He was kicked in the head by a horse the same year and was thought for a brief time to be dead. His education was very limited. He only attended school briefly on a few occasions and then for only a few months at the most.

Everything in Lincoln's early life said that he should be poor and relatively unsuccessful. But he had perseverance and determination. He was determined to become educated in spite of his limited schooling. He borrowed books and read every chance that he got. In 1831, he learned basic math, read Shakespeare and Robert Burns, and began participating in a local debating society.

The next year he became a candidate for the Illinois General Assembly. The Black Hawk War interrupted the campaign, since he served in a rifle company for three months. In August, he lost the election. The store he was working for went out of business. He entered into a partnership to buy another store, which failed the next year and left him badly in debt. In August, 1834, he was finally elected to the Illinois General Assembly as a member of the Whig party. A year later, his partner died and made his debt even worse. In 1836 and 1838, he was reelected to the General Assembly but he still had a bout with severe depression in the middle of it all. In 1837, his courtship of Mary Owens ended when she turned down his proposal. He had another episode with depression in 1840. He married Mary Todd in Springfield. In 1843, he failed in his try for nomination to the U.S. Congress. In 1846, he was elected to the House of Representatives. In 1850, his son died after a two-month illness. In 1855, he failed in a bid to be a U.S. Senator. In 1858, he became the Republican candidate for U.S. Senator from Illinois but lost the vote in the legislature. On November 6, 1860, Abraham Lincoln became one of the most remembered and loved presidents the United States has ever had.[1]

Anyone can succeed. Anyone can become wealthy. The principles are in the Word of God for all who want to look. No matter how great the obstacles or how humble your beginning, no matter how limited your resources, you can gain wealth. Just remember that the thing to do when all else has failed is to try again.

Chapter 10 Summary

Bulldog Tenacity

Building wealth takes time. You have to study business and investments, learn how they work, and keep at it until you are successful. To be wealthy, you must follow these four steps.

1. Plan purposefully.
2. Prepare prayerfully.
3. Proceed positively.
4. Pursue persistently.

Opportunities for investment are unparalleled in America because of the dominance of the baby boomers. They have money and they want to spend it. They don't want to save it. They drive an emotional economy.

The Emotions of Spending

Emotion is energy in motion.

1. The poor are driven by the emotions of fear and greed.
2. The rich are driven by passion and faith.

Knowing this, we can look for appropriate places to invest. The wants and needs of the baby boomers drive the marketplace.

1. Pharmaceuticals are good as long as the company is keeping pace with new developments. Look for companies that have ongoing research and development. Baby boomers want to live forever.
2. Tech stocks are good but can be volatile.
3. Convenience and quality are things that sell. Companies that emphasize premium quality, fast response and delivery times, and personal service are generally successful.

Prejudice Against the Rich

These kinds of investments are really common sense, but we have been so ingrained with religious thinking that we fail to see the opportunities. Religion has caused us to give an inordinate amount of attention to ministering to the poor. We ignore the rich, when they are the ones who finance everything the church does. We have developed a prejudice against the rich.

Jesus only took people with Him who were successful. He ministered to both the rich and the poor, but He told the poor who were saved to go back home and straighten out their lives first.

His Disciples were Successful Businessmen

Jesus never said the rich could not enter the kingdom of God. He only warned against depending on wealth rather than depending on God.

11

Distraction, No Action

WHEN I WAS A CHILD I LOVED TO GET A BOX OF CRACKER JACKS®. Down at the bottom of the box was a little package with a toy in it. It was never anything big, but the thrill of finding out what the surprise was and playing with it was always a treat. One of my favorite toys was a little magnifying glass. It was made of plastic and was cheap, but we could take it to school and on a sunny day we could have some fun with it. In the autumn the leaves would fall and when they were nice and dry we could take that cheap plastic toy and use it to focus the sunlight to a pinpoint. It generated enough heat to start a fire that got us in a lot of trouble. The magnifying glass gave the light focus and multiplied its power.

Science has since learned to focus light into a compact, concentrated beam called a laser. This focused light is so powerful that it can cut through metal. Yet it is really just focused light. The focusing of spiritual light could change the world. Jesus came as the light of the world. When He created His church, He made us into laser lights. His intention was for all of the lesser lights to gather together into a focused spiritual laser that would cut through all of the darkness in the world, an intense light that would set communities on fire for Christ. The devil has tried to keep those lights separated because he knows that there is great power in the focused energy of Christians acting in harmony.

I studied martial arts for many years. We would practice by breaking wood. I could break through one inch of wood with my knuckles, with my fingertips, with my elbow, or with my knee. I could break three inches with my hand. The secret was in focusing all of my energy at the point of contact. I am not talking about some weird spiritual thing. Many attach spiritual aspects to the martial arts, but you don't have to go there. I am describing the act of taking all of the physical energy that my body produced in the process of striking the wood and focusing it at a single point. It is focused attention and it has power.

God often prefaced His commands with a call to pay attention. "If you diligently heed the voice of the Lord your God and do what is right in His sight, give ear to His commandments and keep all His statutes . . ." (Exod. 15:26). In the New Testament, Jesus repeatedly said, "He who has an ear to hear, let him hear." It was another way of saying, "Pay attention. Listen up. Focus your attention on what I am telling you." He wasn't just talking about the ear connected to the brain. Hearing implies a response. How many times have you told one of your children to clean his room. He said, "Yes," but still doesn't do it. Your first question is, "Did you hear me?" Well the sound fell on his ears and he acknowledged it but it did not produce a response, so he really didn't "hear" you.

If you actually hear something, it will prompt you to act accordingly. When you hear something with your heart it will produce action. It will produce behavior. You might be excited about gaining wealth because of all the words you have heard or read up to this point, but no matter how excited you get, if it does not motivate you to actually become financially literate and begin the process of investment, then you have not heard. It hasn't gotten from your head into your heart.

The reason it often doesn't get into your heart is because of all the weeds that have been sown there over the years, all the religious attitudes and wrong perceptions that you have allowed to cloud your thinking. You have gotten all the information but you have lost your focus through the distractions around you. When God says, "Pay attention," He means to focus on the task at hand. If you have read this far,

> Where you allow distraction to affect you, there will be no action.

you have probably gained an understanding of what it takes to gain wealth. Now you need to focus your attention toward actually doing it. Where you allow distraction to affect you, there will be no action.

Focus is power. Without it you can waste tremendous amounts of time. Focus will cost you. You will have to give up something in order to focus your attention on gaining wealth. It will be worth it in the end, but you must focus first. If you spend five hours a night watching television you might have to pull the plug on it so that you have time to read books about the stock market. Television shows are all about people who never watch television. If they watched television, they would never have time to do anything interesting enough to put on television. If you want to succeed, you will have to make some effort. Sitting in your living room and relaxing won't get you there.

Getting Focused . . . and Staying Focused

One of the staff in our church office created a sign for her office area. It says:

Come by and say, "Hi."
Then you must say, "Goodbye."
Although we'd like to be relational and such,

Work and task are a must, must, must—
Yes, we love you just the same,
We hope to see you now and again.

It's not that she wants to be unfriendly. It's just that people who are productive are focused on what they are doing. Then their thoughts are moving in a specific direction and they are suddenly interrupted by a friendly voice that has nothing more important to say than, "Hi. Just thought I'd stop by and say hello." The time required to bring their focus back to the work they were doing is substantial. They have to remember what they were thinking, which usually means backing up to where they started and working through it again, thought by thought, until they find where they left off. It doesn't take very many of these interruptions before a thirty-minute job has dragged on all day.

The Bible is filled with examples of people who allowed distractions to pull them away from their destiny. Adam and Eve had everything going for them in the garden. They walked and talked with God on a daily basis. The temperature was perfect. They didn't have to worry about what to wear each morning. They just got up, walked through a waterfall, and they were ready for the day. But they got distracted by the devil. And that little "harmless" conversation robbed them of paradise and changed the direction of the world.

Cain got distracted along the way and stopped doing what he was supposed to do. Eventually it led to the murder of his brother and the loss of his destiny.

Abraham was distracted by Sarah's maidservant and he had Ishmael. Isaac was distracted by fear and ended up giving his wife over to Abimelech. Moses was distracted by the injustice of an Egyptian toward one of the Hebrews and ended up killing the Egyptian, an act which forced him to live in the wilderness for many years. Achan was distracted by the desire for what belonged to God; he lost his life. Samson was distracted by Delilah and lost his freedom, his eyesight, and ultimately his life. David was distracted by a bath—or rather the sight of Bathsheba in a bath. His distraction caused the loss of a son and created years of strife in the kingdom.

Even Jesus faced distractions. The greatest ones were caused by His closest followers. But He never allowed them to divert Him from His purpose. On occasion He dealt with them pretty harshly. Matthew recorded an incident that occurred late in the earthly ministry of Jesus. He was preparing His disciples for the trial that was coming.

> Even Jesus faced distractions. The greatest ones were caused by His closest followers.

From that time Jesus began to show His disciples that He must go to Jerusalem, and suffer many things from the elders and chief priests and scribes, and be killed, and be raised on the third day. Then Peter took Him aside and began to rebuke Him, saying, "Far be it from You, Lord; this shall not happen to You!" But He turned and said to Peter, "Get behind Me, Satan! You are an offense to Me, for you are not mindful of the things of God, but the things of men." (Matt. 16:21–23)

Notice what it was that Jesus was showing to His disciples. He explained His whole purpose for coming to earth, including His death and His resurrection.

It appears that none of the twelve disciples believed Him when He spoke of the resurrection. None of them waited around after the crucifixion to welcome Him back from the grave. Jesus had to go and find them later. Most of them were off fishing. In fact, Mary seems to be the only one who actually had any belief in His words. The others simply couldn't understand it: "But they did not understand this saying, and were afraid to ask Him" (Mrk. 9:32).

Peter obviously didn't believe it. He had learned one thing from Jesus and that was the power of his confession. So he took Jesus to one side to rebuke Him for being so negative. It seems to me that rebuking the Son of God is kind of dangerous, but Peter was determined and his intentions were good. He assured Jesus that they would protect Him so that nobody could hurt Him. He was not going to let it happen.

Jesus was completely focused on His mission, however. From the time of this incident He began talking about it, explaining what was coming and trying to strengthen His disciples so that they would be ready for it. He spoke of little else during those weeks. He completely immersed Himself and everyone around Him in His destiny. Peter did not understand what was happening. He only listened to part of what Jesus said. He missed the resurrection part of Jesus' words and because of his misperception, he opposed Jesus. He became a distraction to Jesus, trying to get Him to abandon His destiny.

Jesus responded with perhaps the strongest rebuke recorded in the Bible. "Get behind me, Satan." To understand how strong this was, keep the whole picture in mind. Peter was one of the closest disciples to Jesus, one of the inner three, along with James and John. He was thinking about protecting Jesus. In fact, he was declaring that he would lay his own life down to protect Jesus. It is hard to imagine a nobler and more devoted response to the things Jesus had said. And then Jesus called him Satan. How could He be so rude to His most devoted disciple?

First of all, the word in Greek that is used here for Satan is *satanas*. It is transliterated into the name Satan but Jesus was not saying that Peter had turned into the devil or was possessed by the devil. The word simply means "adversary." It is used as a name for the devil because he is "The Adversary," but there is no reason to assume that Jesus was making any reference to the devil in this context.

Rather, He was saying to Peter, "As long as you oppose the

fulfillment of My destiny, you are My adversary." He told Peter to get behind Him because as long as he opposed the destiny that Jesus was walking in, there could be no fellowship between them. Jesus would not be distracted or dissuaded.

Peter was an adversary because his focus was on the things of man, not the things of God. His attention was focused in the wrong place. He became an offense to Jesus. The word "offense" literally means "an occasion to fall." Peter was a distraction which potentially could provide an occasion for Jesus to fall.

It is important to remember that Jesus was one-hundred percent God, but He was also one-hundred percent man. He felt all of the emotions that any of us would feel if we knew we were going to our death. In the garden of Gethsemane, He sweated drops of blood from the pressure He was under. He prayed, "Let this cup pass from Me," because He had no more desire to suffer and die than any of the rest of us would. He had to overcome everything that you and I have been faced with in life. "For we do not have a High Priest who cannot sympathize with our weaknesses, but was in all points tempted as we are, yet without sin" (Heb. 4:15).

> Jesus was one-hundred percent God, but He was also one-hundred percent man.

Jesus was faced with the opportunity to turn back. But He was intensely focused on His destiny. Following it was more important to Him than anything, and if Peter chose to obstruct His path, then Peter was His enemy. Jesus would not let another person change His focus.

There are two important lessons here for us. The first is that once you have set your focus on gaining wealth, you must keep it. There will be many who don't want you to succeed. Some just don't like you. Others mean well. They don't want to see you fail so they try to divert you from your efforts. "Don't get your hopes up," they will say. "You've always been poor and you always will." "Don't take any risks." "Don't be a dreamer."

Well-meaning people can be the most distracting because you know they like you and you don't want to hurt their feelings by ignoring them or disagreeing with them. But if you allow anything that is not in line with the Word of God to influence you, then it will pull you away from your destiny.

In the parable of the sower, it was these kinds of distractions that Jesus had in mind when He talked about the Word being choked out by the cares of this world. Distractions make us lose focus and the Word gets choked before it can bear fruit.

The second lesson is what can be seen in Peter's actions. Be careful that you don't try to affect someone else's focus. Don't rain on their parade. You don't know what God has planned for them. Don't try to discourage them from doing what God has called them to do. Don't be an offense. Don't be the one that provides an occasion for them to fall. Instead, be an encourager. Otherwise you may become God's adversary.

Denying Yourself

Jesus did not stop with His rebuke of Peter. He took the opportunity to teach the disciples something. "Then Jesus said to His disciples, 'If anyone desires to come after Me, let him deny himself, and take up his cross, and follow Me'" (Matt. 16:24).

For two thousand years, men have tried to obey this verse by beating themselves with whips or denying themselves every imaginable physical comfort. They have moved to the desert to live in isolation, in many cases abandoning their wives and children. They have starved themselves on bread and water. Some have even hung themselves on crosses, trying to deny themselves.

The devil loves it when Christians follow this course of action, since people who isolate themselves have no effect on the world around them. They become so distracted by this false understanding of spirituality that they become completely incapable of fulfilling the mission God has for them. Jesus suffered on the cross so that we wouldn't have to. He took the pain so that we could be free of it. Jesus went through the misery so we could live in joy.

What did He mean, then, by "deny himself" and "take up his cross?" For Jesus, His destiny was the cross—and the resurrection. He gave up everything to accomplish His destiny. When He speaks of your cross, He specifically means your destiny. Taking up your cross means to enter into the destiny that God has called you to. Denying yourself means giving up anything that stands in the way of fulfilling your destiny. Denying yourself means not giving in to the distractions that would draw you off of your path.

> Denying yourself means giving up anything that stands in the way of fulfilling your destiny.

What is your destiny? It is not the cross. Jesus did that already so that you could do something else. Your destiny is to fulfill the call of God in your life. For some, that means full-time ministry, but for many more it means starting businesses, making investments, and prospering so that you can be a support to the church where God has placed you.

What does it mean, then, to deny yourself so that you can take up the cross of building the kingdom? It means denying everything that stands in the way of fulfilling your call. It means denying sickness so that you will live longer and do more. It means denying poverty because it is impossible to accomplish very much if you can't afford to even pay your bills and buy food. It means denying yourself the comfort of sitting back with just enough to get by when there is so much work to do in the preaching of the Gospel. If you cannot leave your children's children an inheritance, then you are falling short of building the kingdom.

Jesus emphasized the attitude that His disciples should have in the next few verses.

For whoever desires to save his life will lose it, but whoever loses his life for My sake will find it. For what profit is it to a man if he gains the whole world, and loses his own soul? Or what will a man give in exchange for his soul? For the Son of Man will come in the glory of His Father with His angels, and then He will reward each according to his works. (Matt. 16:25–27)

If you want wealth just so you can move to a cabin in the mountains and relax, then you do not understand God's purpose. That comfort itself will be a distraction that will keep you from your destiny. There is nothing wrong with a cabin in the country and God would love to give you one, but wealth by itself is not the goal and your inactivity is not what God has in mind. Wealth to build God's kingdom is.

Jesus said that He would reward each one according to his works. We know that, in regard to salvation, God considers our righteousness as filthy rags. The works He is talking about are not those that bring us salvation. That can only come from faith in Jesus. The works are those that we do in fulfilling our destiny.

What is the reward? It's not wealth. In heaven, the streets are paved in gold. Money would be meaningless there. The greatest reward we can get is standing before God and hearing Him say, "Well done, good and faithful servant." In order to hear those words, we will need to multiply the seed that God has given us. We share in the wealth and thus build the kingdom. Then, and only then, we will have taken up our cross and followed Jesus.

Chapter 11 Summary

Distraction, No Action

Focused light in the form of a laser is so powerful it can cut through metal. Likewise you have to take your new understanding of how money works and focus it enough to actually do something.

If you really hear something, it will prompt you to action. When God says, "Pay attention," He actually means to focus on the task at hand. Listen and let what you hear drive you to act.

When you allow distraction to affect you, there will be no action.

The Cost of Focus

Focus will cost you. You will have to give up what distracts you from focusing on wealth. It might be television or other activities. It might be acquaintances that use up all of your time.

Jesus faced distractions. His mission was to go to the cross, die, and be resurrected. Peter, one of His closest friends, tried to distract Him by attempting to talk Him out of going to Jerusalem. Peter meant well, but Jesus called Him an adversary, one who provided an occasion to fall. Jesus stayed focused on His mission, however. There are two lessons here:

1. Once you have set your focus on wealth, you must keep it. Many people will try to distract you.
2. Be careful that you don't try to affect someone else's focus.

Jesus took the opportunity to teach His disciples that they should deny themselves and take up their crosses (Matt. 16:24).

1. Taking up your cross means pursuing your destiny.
2. Denying yourself means giving up anything that stands in the way of fulfilling your destiny.

Your destiny is to fulfill the call of God in your life. The reward is achieving wealth so that we can support the building of the kingdom of God.

12

When Going Uphill, Downshift

As you travel south on Interstate 5 in California, there is a lengthy stretch of freeway that runs through the mountains separating central California with the Los Angeles area. It is called the Grapevine. The freeway follows several miles of six and seven percent grades. Steepness of the hill and the great distance from the bottom to the top make the drive difficult for any vehicle. Passenger cars often overheat during the summer. For truck drivers, it is quite a challenge. There are extra lanes just for them so they can make the climb at the expense of speed. They have to downshift in order to get enough power to pull the load up the hill. The engine runs faster, but the gear ratio is lower and the speed is slower. However, the power is so much greater—enough for a truck to climb the mountain and get to the other side.

In gaining wealth, there are some significant mountains that we face. The first is financial literacy. Without gaining an understanding of how money works, you will always be floundering through life, hoping something good will happen but never having any control over it. Having financial literacy means taking control of your direction and not trusting anything to mere chance.

A second mountain is figuring out where the finances are going to come from so that you can invest. You can't start investing and still buy liabilities. If you have a credit card, for example, and you pay off the balance on it every month, then it becomes a useful tool. But if you charge so much that you have no money left over after you have paid it off, then you have not saved anything to invest. You have invested in liabilities instead of assets.

A third mountain is the actual investment process. Too many people try to shortcut the process. They buy stock based on something that someone said or something they heard somewhere. They know nothing about the company or its history. They are just guessing. The process should include research on the company to know as much about it as possible. Then an educated decision can be made regarding the stock investment.

These mountains can be overcome. But you will need to slow down and make sure that you do all of the things necessary to give you the power to get over them. There are no shortcuts. There is no get-rich-quick scheme that will take you to great wealth for your lifetime. You can't just read a couple of books and throw a few dollars into some stock and come out wealthy. There is a process that must be understood and absorbed. You must learn, and learning takes time. Don't rush. Slow down and get it right. Downshift for more power.

> There is no get-rich-quick scheme that will take you to great wealth for your lifetime.

The secret to being rich is not a formula that allows you to invest a certain number of dollars in some specific area and then sit back and wait for the return. Formulas won't work if you have not learned to think, to create opportunities, to evaluate the strengths and weaknesses of potential investments, and to exercise the self-discipline to build your whole lifestyle around assets instead of liabilities. The ability to think is critical.

The Bible explains how to deal with mountains that get in your way.

For assuredly, I say to you, whoever says to this mountain, "Be removed and be cast into the sea," and does not doubt in his heart, but believes that those things he says will be done, he will have whatever he says. Therefore I say to you, whatever things you ask when you pray, believe that you receive them, and you will have them. (Mrk. 11:23–24)

The last consideration we must make in our journey to wealth is the importance of faith in the process. There are always obstacles to achieving anything and wealth is no exception. That is why you need determination and passion and perseverance. But the one ingredient that is always necessary to overcome obstacles is faith.

We know that faith is the substance of things hoped for and the evidence of things not yet seen (Heb. 11:1). Faith means believing that you have something before it can be seen in the natural world. The phrase "believe that ye receive them" in the King James Version is actually in the past tense in the original Greek. It literally means "believe you have received them." With faith, you believe that it is already done before you can see it in the natural. If you have it in the natural, you don't need faith.

I have left the discussion of faith until the end for a couple of reasons. First of all, it is so often misunderstood by Christians. Those who have heard the faith message have convinced themselves that if they just believe hard enough, then money is going to pour out of heaven. If they just tithe, then they are going to suddenly have more money than they know what to do with.

The money doesn't just appear, however. We need to learn to tithe, as this will protect the things we have. Yet it isn't the catalyst that multiplies our seed; instead it keeps the devil away. It is not a matter of fighting the devil. Those who are constantly fighting him to keep their possessions are non-tithers.

We also need to learn to give offerings because that results in blessing on the investments we plant. It causes God to bless our investments. Faith is involved in both of these activities and its importance cannot be overstated. The seed that we plant will come back thirty, sixty, and a hundredfold. But it doesn't come back from the church. It doesn't appear from nowhere. It is the result of God's multiplication of the seed we plant in the storehouse connected to faith. Then the money invested in the earth—our assets—must be multiplied. If nothing is planted in the form of assets, if the only thing planted is the offering into the kingdom, then God has little to work with to multiply.

It is for this reason I have emphasized the need to become financially literate so that you can stop working for money and learn to make money work for you. If you have only faith with no action, there is nothing for your faith to operate on. You have to invest something and it needs to be done in an intelligent manner. Now that you have begun to grasp this concept, however, we can return to a discussion of faith and its importance in the investment process. Your faith has to be connected to what you do. There is a link between what you plant and the harvest that needs to be watered with faith. Your expectation will affect your harvest.

> If you have only faith with no action, there is nothing for your faith to operate on.

As an example of what I mean, look at how the stock market usually operates. The Federal Reserve Board attempts to regulate the economy through various means. A prominent method is by altering interest rates that banks use to lend money to each other. When the rates go up, it is more difficult to get loans and the economy slows down. When the rates go down, loans are easier to obtain and the economy speeds up.

Generally the stock market follows the economy. If the interest rates go up, stocks go down. If the interest rates go down, stocks go up. The Federal Reserve Board was created in 1913. The stated purpose was to "promote effectively the goals of maximum employment, stable prices and moderate long-term interest rates." The actual outcome of it was to provide a vehicle through which the rich could manipulate the stock market in such a way that more money was taken from the hands of the poor and put into the hands of the rich. If the rich can scare enough people into getting out of the stock market then prices will drop and the rich can pick up the same stocks at a low price and hold them until the prices go up.

Without faith, you might panic right along with everyone else. You look at what the newspapers say. You listen to the experts who tell you the market is about to suffer a decline. So we sit and wait in gloom for our stocks to drop. We expect the worst. When faith connects to my investments, however, I begin to realize that God gave me dominion. It doesn't matter what anybody else's stocks are doing. God said that because I am a tither and because I bring offerings, God is obligated to prosper what my hands touch. That means that I can trust Him to lead me to the right stocks in the first place and I can require of Him that the stocks I buy will prosper. By faith I can take dominion and authority over the economy and it must be reconciled to God.

By faith I can buy property and it has to sell at a higher price than what I bought it for. I have planted seed in the kingdom of God and the multiplication must come to my investments.

It doesn't matter what the Federal Reserve Chairman does. It doesn't matter what the economy is doing. It doesn't matter what the Dow Jones is doing. When my faith connects to my investments, then I can expect them to multiply. I can say to those mountains, "Be cast into the sea," and they will have to go. If you believe it and you have received it, then faith will bring it about.

You will not go any further than the vision that you have. Your expectations will be molded by your vision. Are you believing God to get you out of debt? That's good but you need to think bigger. Are you believing for a million dollars? That's better, but why not ten million?

The danger in speaking this way about faith is that you might sit down and have faith and not actually do anything. You must invest and you must work or there is nothing for your faith to connect to. You become like the man who lost his business—in fact lost everything. He was a tither and he gave offerings so he went to God and said, "Lord, just let me win the lottery." Each week he prayed and each week he did not win. Week after week he continued praying, reminding God that he was a tither and still he didn't win. Finally he got mad and shouted, "God, give me a break, will you? Please let me win the lottery." Thunder and lightning came over the church and a booming voice came out of heaven and God said, "Give me a break. Buy a ticket."

I'm not advocating investment in lottery tickets. They are not exactly an investment in assets. But we need a balance between having faith and doing something for the faith to connect to. This is what James meant when he said faith and works went together: "But someone will say, 'You have faith, and I have works.' Show me your faith without your works, and I will show you my faith by my works" (James 2:18).

> If you have faith, then you will not sit and wait.

If you have faith, then you will not sit and wait. You will become financially literate and begin investing so that your faith can connect to something real. God can't bless faith if you haven't put your hand to something. He also can't bless the work of your hands if you don't have faith.

Putting Your Faith into Action

The life of Elisha the prophet gives us an excellent example of faith demonstrated by action. A woman who was in a desperate situation came to him for help. "A certain woman of the wives of the sons of the prophets cried out to Elisha, saying, 'Your servant my husband is dead, and you know that your servant feared the Lord. And the creditor is coming to take my two sons to be his slaves'" (2 Kgs. 4:1).

This was a family that lived by liabilities, not assets. The husband used credit until he was so deeply in debt that his wife was left with nothing but the debt. The debt threatened to take her whole family. He was not a bad man. In fact, what is said about him indicates that he was apparently quite spiritual. He loved God. He was a servant. He had a prophetic ministry. But he was not financially literate.

"So Elisha said to her, 'What shall I do for you? Tell me, what do you have in the house?' And she said, 'Your maidservant has nothing in the house but a jar of oil'" (2 Kgs. 4:2). She didn't have much to start with but God doesn't need much. Your initial investment doesn't have to be large. God will always start with what we have and He will make it enough.

> Then he said, "Go, borrow vessels from everywhere, from all your neighbors—empty vessels; do not gather just a few. And when you have come in, you shall shut the door behind you and your sons; then pour it into all those vessels, and set aside the full ones." So she went from him and shut the door behind her and her sons, who brought the vessels to her; and she poured it out. (2 Kgs. 4:3–5)

Several levels of faith are demonstrated here by the actions of the people involved. Elisha's faith was not in question. He told her to get a bunch of vessels, not just a few. He expected God to do something that would match the woman's faith. Elisha was in the right place.

The woman obviously had some faith since it produced action. She believed what Elisha said enough that she went and did as he instructed. The limits of her faith are shown by her dependence on her sons' faith. She trusted them to bring vessels when she should have gone herself. It got the multiplication of

God started, nevertheless. Still, depending on someone else to do it limited the outcome.

> *Now it came to pass, when the vessels were full, that she said to her son, "Bring me another vessel." And he said to her, "There is not another vessel." So the oil ceased. Then she came and told the man of God. And he said, "Go, sell the oil and pay your debt; and you and your sons live on the rest." (2 Kgs. 4:6–7)*

The multiplication stopped when the woman ran out of places to put it. Her faith was demonstrated in the degree to which she prepared for the blessing. The level of blessing was decided before the oil began to multiply. She should have collected every vessel in the city. She got many but she could have done even more. Her investment was in the form of vessels collected. She gathered enough to get her through the recession. She was able to pay off her debts and live for a time on the remainder.

You must have faith to prosper. Each step that you take in the process of gaining wealth demonstrates your level of faith. Sitting and waiting doesn't get you very far, no matter how strongly you believe. Tithing is a step of faith that says you believe God will protect what you have. Offerings above and beyond your tithes are a step of faith that says you believe God will prosper and multiply the work of your hands. The effort of becoming financially literate, that is, educating yourself, is a step of faith that demonstrates how far you will allow God to go in multiplying your investment. It's like collecting vessels. The more you learn about how money works, the more vessels you have. The blessings of God will only go as far as your preparation to receive them.

> Sitting and waiting doesn't get you very far, no matter how strongly you believe.

What God really wants is for you to never stop preparing. Keep collecting vessels for the rest of your life so He can keep pouring out blessings for the rest of your life. The actual investment you make is like pouring out the oil. It is the last step in the process and the culminating step of faith. The more you invest, the more you will have. Never stop investing and never stop learning. Financial literacy is not just a matter of reading a couple of books; it is a way of life. Abundance is not having many possessions. It is a lifestyle.

God is interested in doing so much more than just meeting your needs. As He tells us in Philippians 4:19, "And my God shall supply all your need according to His riches in glory by Christ Jesus." The term "glory" is interchangeable with "power" in the New Testament. Jesus is the Word. Another way of saying this is that God will supply your needs according to His riches in the power of His Word. How abundantly your needs are met depends on how much the Word of God is working in your life.

There are Christians who are losing their houses and ending up on the street. Their car is repossessed. They have to get food at the church because they can't afford groceries. I am not being judgmental of their situation, but I am saying that their faith has not connected enough to the power of the Word. If the Word is working in you, it will produce faith, since faith comes by hearing the Word. If faith is there, then it will produce action and you will begin tithing. You will bring offerings. You will begin investing. And God will meet every need with so much you won't know what to do with it all. Ephesians 3:20 links God's power to our ability to think—"Now to Him who is able to do exceedingly abundantly above all that we ask or think, according to the power that works in us."

The New International Version translates this verse as "more than all we ask or imagine." The only limit on how much God can do is you. How much can you imagine? How many vessels can you collect? The power of the Word is more than able to bring you more than you can imagine. John wrote a very quotable verse: "Beloved, I pray that you may prosper in all things and be in health, just as your soul prospers" (3 John 2).

We love this promise. We usually only take this as far as saying that we will prosper according to how our soul prospers. But there is a contingency. John said, "I pray." We have a responsibility to pray, particularly those in leadership. Prosperity doesn't just happen because your soul is saved. There must be action prompted by faith, connected to the power of the Word. An expanded translation of this verse might sound more like this:

> *Friends, I pray you, through all and every situation, to have success in business affairs, and reaching all goals concerning prosperity, and with this, that you have sound health because you're true to Bible doctrine and thus you will increase financially according to and in measurement with the vitality of your heart's desire to succeed and to increase in wealth.*

Vitality means "physical and mental vigor." Is the vigor of your heart's desire causing you to stand in faith for just enough or do you believe too much? Ultimately the answer to that question will determine your destiny.

Chapter 12 Summary

When Going Uphill, Downshift

In order to get enough power to climb a mountain, truck drivers have to downshift. They have to slow down. There are mountains that have to be climbed in order to achieve wealth.

1. You have to have financial literacy. You have to learn how money and business work.
2. You have to find money to invest.
3. You have to actually invest in something, which means you have to do some research about the company or business that you are considering investing in.

To overcome these mountains, you have to downshift, slow down. There are no shortcuts to wealth. There is a process that has to be understood and absorbed. There is no formula. You have to be able to think.

The Role of Faith

Faith is an essential component of success in overcoming obstacles.

Faith means believing that you have something before it can be seen in the natural world.

Faith doesn't mean you just believe and you will become rich. Tithing protects your possession. Offerings bring a spiritual blessing. But you still have to make an investment or there is nothing to bless. Faith produces action.

Your faith has to be connected to what you do. There is a link between what you plant and the harvest that needs to be watered with faith. Your expectation will affect your harvest.

1. If you invest in stocks, your faith will keep you from panicking when everyone else does. Your faith can affect your stock's performance.
2. By faith, you can buy property and it has to sell at a higher price than you bought it for.

You will not go any further than the vision you have. Your expectations, your faith, will be molded by your vision.

You need a balance between having faith and doing something for faith to connect to. Faith without work is dead. Show your faith by your actions.

The story of Elisha and the widow (2 Kgs. 4:1–7) illustrates the connection of faith and action.

1. Elisha instructed her to gather as many containers as she could, and then to pour her small supply of oil into them.
2. The oil didn't run out until there were no more containers to pour into. The level of her faith was determined by how many containers she and her sons gathered.

13

Jesus Wasn't Poor

ABOUT THE YEAR AD 270, A MAN NAMED ANTONY FORSOOK ALL THE comforts of society and moved to the desert of Egypt to serve God through a life of solitude. For the next fifteen years, he scratched out an existence in complete isolation and abject poverty. He believed that his lifestyle was an imitation of Jesus and the ideal He presented. He was absolutely convinced that Jesus was poor and that to become perfect—as Jesus was perfect—he must become poor as well.

Antony was part of a very popular movement in which thousands believed they would please God by removing themselves as far as possible from contact with other people and spending their time praying and fasting. These men gave away all of their possessions, which was not much in most cases. They lived on the meager income that came from making things like baskets and mats. Their entire diet consisted of bread or roots and wild plants that could be gathered nearby. They existed in complete destitution—all for the glory of God.

For nearly two thousand years, Antony and others like him have been regarded by much of the world as devout and holy men

192 ~ Dr. C. Thomas Anderson

of God. Even today, when few would ever consider living such a life themselves, some Christians still think those men were particularly devoted to God, and the self-denial of a life of poverty is still held up as an ideal of spiritual attainment.

The problem with this adoration is that it has no basis in Scripture or in the history of the first church. So many assume that Jesus lived a life of poverty that they never question where this concept came from. Those who seek wealth often feel a little guilty about it, believing that they are somehow not doing God's perfect will if they have too much money. They often think of themselves as second class Christians, not as worthy or as spiritual as those who have renounced worldly gain.

This kind of thinking has prevented many Christians from ever becoming what God created them to be or accomplishing what God called them to accomplish. It is a mindset that has to be dealt with if you want to attain success in life.

The ideal of poverty is not based on Scripture. It came from an entirely different source, and we need to recognize it for what it is. The New Testament church did not espouse poverty. The earliest disciples were not poor men, and Jesus was not poor. He did not change the world by wandering through the countryside with a ragged group of beggars, avoiding the sinners of the world and preaching that everyone should become destitute and wretched. The belief that the Bible teaches poverty did not originate with Jesus. It crept into the church at least a hundred years later. Once it was generally accepted as truth, people searched for Scripture to support it and to justify their own lack. But to do that, they had to take many verses out of context and twist their meanings, and they had to ignore the multitude of passages that speak of the abundant life of the kingdom of God.

Nearly every school of Greek philosophy held a common belief that all physical matter was inherently flawed. Consequently, only that which was spirit could be perfect. Since matter was flawed, it was impossible for anyone to ever obtain perfection while in a physical body. Likewise, anything that was part of the physical world was inferior to the things of the spiritual world. In many schools of thought, this translated into the idea that if you wanted to be good, you had to separate yourself completely from anything to do with the world—from pleasure of any kind, from money and possessions, and from contact with anyone who sought pleasure.

This view was never biblical, but within the first three centuries of the early church, many of the concepts of Greek thinking were assimilated into Christian doctrine. The change was subtle, but it was very real and it has crippled the church ever since.

To some degree, it is understandable that people made the association between suffering and righteousness. From the beginning, enemies of the church persecuted, tortured, and killed Christians. We have all heard stories of the Roman Empire in which believers were thrown to the lions or burned at the stake. Not all of the Roman emperors did so, but many were determined to eliminate all the followers of Christ from society. Nero and Domitian are two prominent examples.

Those who refused to denounce Christ, even when faced with death, were held up as heroes of faith. It wasn't long before martyrdom itself became elevated in people's minds as the ideal of Christian service. People began to equate martyrdom with Christian perfection and if they weren't being persecuted, they felt that they were somehow slacking in their devotion. Things became so unbalanced that many considered it better to die for Christ than to live for Him. It wasn't a very big step to go from revering the suffering of martyrdom to revering the suffering of poverty.

How destructive this tendency was to the life and the mission of the church became evident after Constantine converted to Christianity. Suddenly it was legal to believe in Jesus. Persecution came to an abrupt end.

Unfortunately, by that time, most of the church had come to believe the Greek position that anything physical or pleasurable was bad. This belief combined with the feeling that you weren't really serving God if you weren't being persecuted. Instead of enjoying the new freedom of tolerance and using it as an opportunity for proclaiming their faith openly, people began to feel guilty about not suffering. They believed that they had to distance themselves from the material world, contrary to what Jesus had really taught. They began to look for ways they could inflict suffering upon themselves. A life of poverty was just one of the many ways religious minds of the day found to restrict life so that it would never become too abundant or too enjoyable. This self-destructive, religious mindset of "suffering is good" converged with the infusion of Greek philosophy to produce a climate of poverty that has not left the church since.

It all sounds very noble on the surface. Renounce the things of the world. Avoid contact with sin or with sinners, and thereby remain pure and uncontaminated. They based their beliefs on a handful of Bible verses taken out of context. Matthew 19:21 was a favorite:

If you want to be perfect, go, sell what you have and give to the poor, and you will have treasure in heaven.

In that passage, of course, Jesus was speaking directly to a wealthy young man who was completely controlled by his money. The lesson Jesus wanted to convey was not, "Become poor," but rather, "Do not let your money control you."

To stay away from money and from other temptations, the early monks emphasized the importance of isolation. The less contact you had with other people, the better. They carried it so far that they came to believe a truly spiritual person would not even notice other people or the temptations they might bring. One story is told of a monk who had to walk into a nearby town. On the way, he met a group of nuns who were traveling in the opposite direction. He moved off the path to let them by, but their superior said to him, "If you were a perfect monk, you would not have looked at us and you would not have seen that we were women."

The result of all this "holiness" was not the spread of the Gospel. It was rather a complete shunning of responsibility and accountability. The worst kinds of abuse were essentially blamed on God, who the monks believed had commanded the poverty and seclusion. Many of the men who sought isolation in the desert left behind wives and children who were often thrown into the streets without the means to support themselves, since their husbands abandoned them to serve God in the desert. In the communities of monks that developed, all kinds of perverse activities were reported—not by enemies of the monks, but by the monks themselves. Many young boys who came to the desert were sexually abused. Women in the local towns were a constant source of pleasure—often without their own consent—for those monks who could not get over their sinful tendencies.

What was missing from all of this "holy" living was any understanding of just what it was that God actually wanted people to be doing in His service. Jesus really left no doubt. His last instructions were clear.

> *Go into all the world and preach the Gospel to every creature.* (Mrk. 16:15)

It should be obvious that fulfilling this command requires meeting people and talking to them. "Go into all the world" cannot possibly be interpreted as, "Isolate yourself from everyone in the world." "Preach the Gospel" cannot be interpreted as "Avoid all sinners." There is nothing holy about avoiding people. According to the Bible, it is both selfish and foolish.

> There is nothing holy about avoiding people.

A man who isolates himself seeks his own desire;
He rages against all wise judgment. (Prov. 18:1)

It should also be obvious that you cannot "go into all the world" if you are broke. Without money, you cannot even go to the store, much less the city, or the state, or the rest of the country. Ministry takes money. Just as isolation is a selfish belief, so is poverty. If you do not seek prosperity, you limit the spreading of the Gospel to the world and you are limiting you and your family from the larger blessing God has for you.

This is why it is so important that we develop a healthy understanding of the life and ministry of Jesus. He never had a problem with money. He had plenty of it, and He knew how to use it properly. It is time we look at some of these fallacies and lay them to rest.

Jesus Became Poor to Make Us Rich

First of all, consider the larger concepts that are involved. Jesus became poor only once in His life—for the three hours that He was on the cross. He became poor to make us rich.

For you know the grace of our Lord Jesus Christ, that though He was rich, yet for your sakes He became poor, that you through His poverty might become rich. (2 Cor. 8:9)

Opponents of prosperity will try to say that this verse refers to being rich in spiritual blessings, not in money. But in the next chapter, Paul clarified what he meant by "rich."

While you are enriched in everything for all liberality, which causes thanksgiving through us to God. (2 Cor. 9:11)

The New International Version is even more direct. It translates this verse with the words, "You will be made rich in every way so that you can be generous on every occasion." Whichever way you translate it, "Enriched in everything," or, "made rich in every way," includes more than just spiritual blessings. It means *every* way, including money. Jesus became poor to make us rich in every way.

> Jesus became poor
> to make us rich
> in every way.

Poverty falls short of the blessing power of God. In Hebrew, blessing means health, wealth, joy, peace, and highly favored (Gen. 1:28). Therefore, poverty was born on the cross to undo what Adam and Eve lost in the garden. Poverty was part of the sin Jesus took on Himself in order to set us free. Everything that hinders us from life, He carried to the grave and left there.

> *Surely He has borne our griefs*
> *And carried our sorrows;*
> *Yet we esteemed Him stricken,*
> *Smitten by God, and afflicted.*
> *But He was wounded for our transgressions,*
> *He was bruised for our iniquities;*
> *The chastisement for our peace was upon Him,*
> *And by His stripes we are healed.*
> (Isa. 53:4–5)

During the three hours that Jesus hung on the cross, He experienced all the sickness, sorrow, hate, pain, poverty, suffering, and disease in the world so that He could replace each of those things with the life God wanted us to have. He became sin on our behalf.

For He made Him who knew no sin to be sin for us, that we might become the righteousness of God in Him. (2 Cor. 5:21)

He became hate so we can know love.
He became sorrow so we can know joy.
He became sin so we can have righteousness.
He became poor so we can become rich in every way.

The Word Is Not Poor

The first chapter of John tells us that Jesus is the Word of God and that the Word became flesh and lived in our midst. Jesus, the Word, never did without anything. He had all the resources of the universe at His disposal. The only time He did not use those resources was on the cross. Even then, He could have called on them if He chose to. At the time of His arrest in Gethsemane, He told His disciples that He could call on the Father and have twelve legions of angels there if He chose to. The Word was filled with the power of God to accomplish anything. He was the express image of the Father.

> If Jesus is not poor, then neither are we.

Has in these last days spoken to us by His Son, whom He has appointed heir of all things, through whom also He made the worlds; who being the brightness of His glory and the express image of His person, and upholding all things by the word of His power. (Heb. 1:2–3)

If Jesus was the express image of the Father, then He could not have been poor. If you think He was, then your perception of God is limited. If you see Jesus as poor, you see God as poor. If you see God as poor, then you will automatically think of Him as weak and powerless. And the truth is that God is neither weak nor powerless and He is certainly not poor. He owns everything there is. If the Father is not poor, then Jesus is not poor either.

If Jesus is not poor, then neither are we. We are now joint heirs with Jesus (Rom. 8:17). We have access to the same resources Jesus did. He has placed us side by side with Jesus so we can experience the same blessings.

> *Even when we were dead in trespasses, made us alive together with Christ (by grace you have been saved), and raised us up together; and made us sit together in the heavenly places in Christ Jesus.* (Eph. 2:5–6)

Notice the verb tense in that statement. We have been raised. It is not something that we are waiting to get to heaven to experience. It is an accomplished fact now. The Word is not poor, and as long as we are followers of the Word, we are not poor either.

The Life of Jesus

The popular conception of Jesus as poor has given birth to some images that are so ingrained in our thinking that we rarely question them. The Bible doesn't directly state, "Jesus was not poor," but there are many indications of it, if we just take the time to think about them. I offer here a few examples to demonstrate that Jesus was not born into poverty and He did not live in poverty.

Jesus Was Born to the Lineage of David

Jesus was born into a family with a better than average social standing. Mary and Joseph were both from the royal lineage of King David. Both of the genealogies of Jesus (Matt. 1:1–17 and Luk. 3:23–37) demonstrate Mary and Joseph's heritage. This alone would have conferred some degree of status, but more important,

Mary's family was directly connected to the priesthood, at least on her mother's side, since her cousin Elizabeth was the wife of a priest, Zacharias. This implies that Mary's family had a high social standing because the custom of the day would not sanction a priest marrying someone not from a priestly family unless they held high status. Jesus was born into a family that understood high society, and He learned early in life how to conduct Himself properly when around those who were wealthy and influential. We know that He later spent a great deal of time attending the most prestigious banquets given by the social elite of every town He went to.

In Nazareth, where Jesus grew up, that priestly standing would have been especially significant. Nazareth was not a large town at the time of Christ, probably no more than five hundred people, but it did sit on a main trade route between the seaports of the Mediterranean coast and Damascus, by way of Capernaum. As such, steady traffic from all over the world passed through the town. Part of that traffic was connected to the ministry of the Temple.

The priests lived all over Israel. They were divided into twenty-four sections called courses. Only one course served in the Temple at a time, each acting for a period of one week and taking turns, so that each course served twice a year. When it was time to travel to Jerusalem for their regular duty, the priests of a course gathered in one of several towns that served as meeting points and then traveled to Jerusalem together. Nazareth was one of those priest centers. Anyone connected to the priesthood, as Jesus' family was, would have been held in relatively higher honor because of the significance of the priesthood in Nazareth.

This is our first clue to understanding Jesus and the social standing of His family.

The Inn Was Full

The second point deals with the birth of Jesus and the circumstances surrounding it. Most people today picture a poverty-stricken Mary and Joseph, unable to find a place to stay for the night and forced into a manger located in a cave. At Christmas, we love to sing about what has become the popular image. "Away in a manger, no crib for a bed, the little Lord Jesus laid down His sweet head." It is a quaint picture of the humble birth of the Savior of the world.

The problem with this nostalgic image is that it ignores most of the facts. Mary and Joseph did not go to the manger because they couldn't afford an inn. They went because there was no room in the inn (Luk. 2:7). I have no doubt that Mary mentioned to Joseph, "I can't believe you didn't make a reservation!"

Mary and Joseph Had a House in Bethlehem

They spent the night of Jesus' birth in a stable because it was the only place available. But they didn't stay there. When the Magi arrived from the East, they didn't go to the manger. They went to a house:

> And when they had come into the house, they saw the young Child with Mary His mother, and fell down and worshiped Him. (Matt. 2:11)

Obviously, Joseph moved the family to better lodgings as soon as they were available. He was prosperous enough to make the move.

The Magi Brought Expensive Gifts

Even if Mary and Joseph were poor up to that time, they certainly weren't poor after the Magi visited. The gifts they brought were items fit for a king:

> And when they had opened their treasures, they presented gifts to Him: gold, frankincense, and myrrh. (Matt. 2:11)

Nativity scenes portray the Magi kneeling before a manger with the shepherds by their side. As we already learned, the Magi did not come to the manger. They arrived quite a bit later. They left their home country when Jesus was born, but they were on the road for a long time. We can get an idea of how long by putting together several of the circumstances given in Matthew.

The night Jesus was born, a star appeared and the Magi followed it to the birthplace. They came first to Jerusalem and spoke with Herod, who was alarmed to learn that a king had been born. He was determined to kill this child before He could grow old enough to take the throne away from Herod and his family.

Herod asked two key questions. In Matthew 2:4–6, he asked the Jewish scholars where the Christ would be born. They looked in the Scriptures and found that Bethlehem was the city.

From the wise men, he learned the time when the star appeared (Matt. 2:7). It was this information that caused him to later kill all the children in Bethlehem that were under two years old. If the star appeared when Jesus was born, then the Magi had been on the road for as long as two years. Even allowing for time to prepare for the trip, they certainly had been traveling for at least one year and more likely a year and a half.

It shouldn't take much thought to realize that a group of foreign dignitaries doesn't travel more than a year to present a baby rattle or a pacifier. They brought gifts appropriate for a king. They brought gold, which has always been valuable in every culture at any time in history. They brought frankincense, a highly valued kind of incense. They brought myrrh, a resin that was used in perfumes and incense. At the time of Christ, it was likely more valuable by weight than gold. Those were not cheap gifts.

We are not told the quantities of any of those substances, but no one traveled for that long to hand over a single gold coin and a pinch of powder. The amounts had to be substantial. Whatever the financial state of Mary and Joseph prior to the visit, they had plenty of money afterward.

Jesus Was Well Educated

In Luke 2:41–50, an incident is described in which Joseph and Mary lost Jesus in Jerusalem. They were there for the Passover celebration with a large group of family and friends. On the return journey, after a day of travel, they realized Jesus was not with them, and they spent the next three days trying to find Him. When they did, Jesus was in the Temple courtyard "sitting in the midst of the teachers, both listening to them and asking them questions" (verse 46).

A poor ragamuffin twelve-year-old child would not have been allowed to sit in the Temple with the greatest teachers of Israel for three days. They not only tolerated His presence, but they were "amazed" at His understanding and His answers. Jesus was well educated. Only the well-to-do could afford schooling. A homeless child would not be welcomed in the Temple, much less be allowed to speak.

Jesus' First Miracle Was a Miracle of Luxury, Performed in a Setting of Prosperity

The Gospel of John records the first miracle Jesus performed. It was at a wedding in the town of Cana in Galilee. As the banquet progressed, the host ran out of wine to serve his guests and Jesus' mother asked Him to help (John 2:3).

Jesus told the servants to fill some large containers with water and serve it to the guests. When they did so, the water turned into wine. John 2:11 says that this was the "beginning of signs Jesus did."

Notice that Jesus was invited to a pretty big wedding. This is another indication of the social standing He held. Cana was a very upscale area. The miracle itself indicates that the family hosting the wedding was wealthy. The embarrassment over running out of wine implies that this was a family of high social standing. Otherwise, it would not have been such a problem. Only the rich would have been invited. The fact that Jesus and His mother were

204 ~ Dr. C. Thomas Anderson

there implies that they were wealthy enough to be included in higher social circles.

Also, notice that there was no practical reason for the miracle. No one would have died if the party ran out of wine. Jesus did not heal anyone or cast out a demon or raise anyone from the dead. He provided the means for the celebration to continue. That is a peculiar thing for someone to do who is preaching poverty and separation from anything pleasurable. Jesus was not only accustomed to hanging out with wealthy people, He clearly had no problem with their celebrations or with the enjoyment of that wealth.

The Disciples Were Successful Businessmen

Not long after the wedding at Cana, Jesus called upon twelve men to become His disciples and follow Him. It is interesting to note that not one of the Twelve came out of an unemployment line. They all had businesses and they were all successful.

Peter, Andrew, John, and James all had fishing businesses. They were hard at work when Jesus called them (Matt. 4:18–22). Matthew was a tax collector (Matt. 9:9), a trade known for the wealth of its practitioners.

These were men who understood money and understood business. Jesus did not surround Himself with men who were poor. He purposely sought out men who had already proven they had the attitude and the mentality necessary to be productive in life.

> Jesus did not surround Himself with men who were poor.

Imagine for a moment what the calling of the disciples would have looked like if Jesus really was poor. Jesus is baptized in the River Jordan in Matthew 3:13–17. Immediately after that, He is led into the wilderness where He fasts for forty days (Matt. 4:1–11). He sleeps in the dirt. His hair, already disheveled from the baptism, now has burrs in it from sleeping on the ground. He is homeless, pushing a shopping cart filled with aluminum cans, and His clothes are soiled and tattered. Jesus shuffles along the shoreline of the Sea of Galilee where He sees the working wealthy businessmen. He signals them with a wave and says, "Come follow Me and I will make you fishers of men," and they drop everything and follow Him.

This is the depiction that many believe without realizing how ludicrous it is. It is an image that is completely contrary to human nature.

The rich follow the rich.
The poor follow the rich.
But the rich don't follow the poor.

Jesus came by the Sea of Galilee looking good and blessed, dressed in an Armani suit, Bruno Magli shoes, and when He said, "Follow me," they were so impressed that they dropped everything and followed Him. We know Jesus dressed well because at the cross they gambled for His clothes, including His one-piece, woven undergarment.

The Disciples Didn't Question Jesus' Ability to Spend a Fortune

One of the best known miracles Jesus performed was the feeding of the five thousand. Most are familiar enough with the story that we don't need to look at all the details here. Large crowds followed Jesus into a remote place and listened to Him teach all day. At some point, the disciples came to Jesus and told Him that He needed to let the people leave so they could go find food in the surrounding villages. Jesus told His disciples to feed the multitude themselves and then took five small loaves of bread and two fish and broke them into pieces. As the disciples distributed the food, it multiplied until all five thousand men plus the women and children were fed.

What is interesting is the reaction of the disciples to Jesus' suggestion that they should feed the people:

But He answered and said to them, "You give them something to eat." And they said to Him, "Shall we go and buy two hundred denarii worth of bread and give them something to eat?" (Mrk. 6:37)

They were shocked that Jesus might want to spend that much money for a single meal, but they also asked if He really wanted them to do it. That implies that they could have paid, meaning that Jesus had quite a bit of money on hand. If Jesus was broke, their question would have been ridiculous.

Jesus Needed a Treasurer to Keep Track of the Money

As a corollary to the last point, Jesus had large amounts of money that He dispersed. He traveled with a pretty large group of people. It wasn't just the twelve. They were the central core of Jesus' followers, but they weren't the only ones by any means. That number grew to at least seventy as Jesus attracted other disciples (Luk. 10:1). In addition, there were a number of women who traveled with Him (Luk. 8:1–3; 23:49). Food alone required a considerable investment every week. There was enough money involved that Jesus appointed one of the twelve to handle it. The job fell to Judas (John 13:29). Whenever Jesus wanted something purchased, He sent Judas to take care of it. If Jesus lived in poverty, it is odd that He needed someone to take care of the money box for Him.

Jesus Could Pour a Year's Wages on the Ground and Not Miss It

Near the end of His ministry, Jesus was at the home of Simon the leper in the town of Bethany. While they were sitting there, something happened that provoked complaints from Jesus' own disciples that He was wasting money on great and needless extravagance.

> *A woman came to Him having an alabaster flask of very costly fragrant oil, and she poured it on His head as He sat at the table.* (Matt. 26:7)

The disciples were indignant, especially Judas, who pointed out how valuable the oil was. It could have been sold for the equivalent of a year's wages and given to the poor! In modern terms, that meant it was worth more than forty thousand dollars.

For Jesus, however, it was no big deal. He commended the woman for doing a good thing:

> *Why do you trouble the woman? For she had done a good work for Me. For you have the poor with you always, but Me you do not have always.* (Matt. 26:10–11)

Jesus did not seem to think He should give away every penny He had to support the poor. He knew that no matter how much He gave them, they would continue to be poor because they chose to remain poor instead of believing the word of prosperity. Jesus was so comfortable with wealth that He did not flinch at the idea of extravagant demonstrations and He did not feel compelled to give money to those who would not believe for it and work for it.

In many churches today, when someone pulls into the parking lot in a new Mercedes or a Range Rover, people say, "Wow. They could have helped a lot of poor people with that money."

That is a Judas spirit. You, too, can have prosperity and help even more poor people than you ever could if you were poor.

Biblical Prosperity

These are just a few of the little things that we so often miss when we read the Gospels. The truth is that Jesus was not poor. He appealed to the wealthy and to the poor alike. If He had been poor, He would not have appealed to the wealthy. The fact that He moved in every level of society indicates that He must have been part of the wealthiest class.

Jesus called us to carry on the ministry of preaching the Gospel to the world. By looking at the example He set for us, it should become clear that we cannot do that without constantly improving our position in society and the extent of our influence. You will never do that by taking a vow of poverty. The only thing poverty accomplishes is to remove you from having a real impact. Poverty does not spread the Gospel. It spreads only despair and hopelessness.

> Poverty does not spread the Gospel. It spreads only despair and hopelessness.

In the Garden of Eden, I believe we see a symbolic picture of what God considers the Gospel to be about. The land of Eden is a picture of the church. The Garden was placed inside of Eden. The river of Eden, representing the life that comes from God, flowed through the Garden and branched into four rivers. They represent the Gospel that is to flow from the church to the world with the life of God. Each river has a specific meaning.

The first is the Pishon, which means wealth or prosperity. It flowed through the land of Havilah where there was gold. The Pishon represents increase.[1]

Second is the Gihon, a name that means "burst forth, gushing forth." It represents the bursting forth from the bondage of sin. The Gihon pictures salvation.[2]

The third river is the Hiddekel, the Hebrew name for the Tigris. It means "rapid," conveying the idea of the quick flight of an arrow and the swift striking of the target. It is a successful shot. It represents success.[3]

The fourth river is the Euphrates, a Greek form of the Hebrew word *perat*. It means "fruitful." The Euphrates represents redeemed time, or time that becomes fruitful instead of wasted.[4]

The image of the four rivers gives us a clear picture of the Gospel—a moving life force that proceeds from God, through the church, to the family, and flows out to the world in the form of prosperity, salvation, success, and redeemed time.

If you think of the Gospel as simply a matter of people being born again so they can go to heaven, you have left out three-fourths of its meaning. The Gospel declares that God wants you to be born again, experience increase, and be successful and effective with your time. Without all of those elements in your life, you will never have any significant effect on the world.

The damage of the message "Jesus was poor" has hindered the work of the Gospel for two thousand years. It is time to change. God wants the church to prosper, and He wants His children to prosper in order to build His kingdom.

Chapter 13 Summary

Jesus Wasn't Poor

The religious belief that Jesus was poor is not a biblical concept. It came to the church from the influence of Greek philosophy, the belief that anything made of physical matter was inherently flawed. To achieve perfection, you had to escape the physical world and become completely spiritual.

When the church embraced this idea, it attached itself to the idea that if you were not suffering, then you were not spiritual. After the persecution of the church ended, people began to look for other ways to inflict suffering on themselves. The idea of renouncing all worldly possessions and living in poverty was then held up as the ideal of serving God. It comes to us today in the form of the belief that Jesus was poor.

Unfortunately, the more people isolated themselves, the less the Gospel was preached and the more the world slipped into darkness.

Jesus was poor only for the three hours on the cross, when He became poor so that we might become rich (2 Cor. 8:9).

1. He became hate so we can know love.
2. He became sorrow so we can know joy.
3. He became sin so we can have righteousness.
4. He became poor so we can become rich.

Jesus was the Word of God, and the Word cannot be poor. The Word is the power of life and the restoration that overcomes the world. The Gospels show Jesus was not poor, based simply on an observation of His life.

1. Jesus was born of the lineage of David. Mary and Joseph both had high social standing because of their connection to the royal line and because of their connection to the priesthood. They would have been highly regarded.
2. The only reason Jesus was born in a manger was because the inn was full. It was not because they couldn't afford to stay there.
3. Mary and Joseph did not stay in the stable. They got a house after Jesus was born (Matt. 2:11).
4. The gifts the Magi brought were the most expensive and valuable items available at the time—gold, frankincense, and myrrh. They were gifts fit for a king. The Magi would not have traveled that far to bring gifts that were of no value.
5. Jesus was well educated, not a ragamuffin street urchin. He was allowed into the circles of the greatest and most respected scholars of Israel. Only the wealthy had access to the level of education He possessed at the age of twelve.
6. The first miracle was a miracle of luxury, performed in a setting of prosperity. Cana was a wealthy area, and Jesus would not have been invited to such a well-to-do gathering as the wedding if He was poor.
7. The disciples were successful businessmen. Jesus did not call upon people who were standing in the unemployment line. He called those who had proven themselves to be resourceful and able to bring increase.
8. The disciples did not question Jesus' ability to spend enough money to feed five thousand men. He performed a miracle when He fed the five thousand, but when He first suggested that the disciples feed them, they assumed that

He meant to go and buy food. They would not have made that assumption if there was not enough money on hand to do it.

9. Jesus needed a treasurer to keep track of money. Judas filled that role, which would have been completely unnecessary if they were poor. In addition, Judas was able to steal money from the ministry funds without them being missed. If there was not much there, it would have become obvious that something was wrong.

10. The woman with the alabaster jar of perfume poured a year's wages on the ground and Jesus wasn't bothered by it. He didn't feel that it should have been spent on the poor. Such extravagance did not bother Him.

The Gospel message, as Jesus preached it, included a restoration of wealth to God's people. That is the only way God's people can preach the Gospel effectively. It takes money to go into all the world.

14

Becoming Financially Literate

BY THIS TIME, YOU SHOULD BE CONVINCED OF AT LEAST FOUR BASIC points:

1. God wants you to be prosperous.
2. You have to do something—invest—if you want to be prosperous.
3. If you invest God's way, He will multiply your efforts.
4. You must become financially literate before you begin investing.

Of these four points, it is essential that you do not overlook the fourth. Over the past century, the preaching of the prosperity message has resulted in millions of people embracing the first three points but not understanding that the fourth point is absolutely necessary. You must become financially literate. Read. Study. Get in tune with the economy. You have to un-

> If you invest
> God's way, He will
> multiply your efforts.

derstand how the economy works. By the time you hear a news story, it's a week old. When you read a magazine article, it's a month old.

In the long term, this means you will have to develop new habits. Changing what you do with your spare time is a good place to start. Instead of spending every evening after work watching television, begin to set aside time on a daily basis to improve your financial understanding.

Begin to read regularly any book you can find on the stock market, on real estate, on investing, or on anything that deals with the economy. Become familiar with the terminology of business and money. Learn the language.

Subscribe to magazines and newspapers that focus on business and investment. The most obvious are publications such as *The Wall Street Journal*, but there are dozens of periodicals that are available. Just visit a local news stand and start browsing.

Becoming financially literate will mean changing the way you think, and that is a process. The sooner you begin, the better.

There are things you can do immediately, however, that will give you relatively quick results:

Reduce Real Debt

If it's worth more than you owe, it's an asset. Another way of saying this is, if you can sell it for more than you owe, you have an asset. But if its value is so low that you would lose money selling it, it is considered "real debt" and should be avoided. If you already have real debt, you need to eliminate it as quickly as possible.

> Buy one man's junk and turn it into your treasure.

You can do this by taking a second job and paying down the debt until you have the cash flow necessary to begin investing. It is impossible to invest if you have no cash. And it is difficult to find cash when you are overwhelmed by real debt.

You can start as small as five dollars per week at a park-and-swap. It is an old saying that one man's junk is another man's treasure. Buy one man's junk and turn it into your treasure. Fix it, clean it up, paint it, and resell it. Invest five dollars a week for twelve weeks—a total investment of sixty dollars. Then hold a garage sale of your own, double the prices, and you will have $120.

Don't run out and spend that money on lunch, however. Reinvest it, and buy more items. You will soon have enough cash to move to larger items of personal interest. Buy, restore, and resell. Multiply your money as often as you can and you will find that you can generate a million dollars in three years from an initial investment of just sixty dollars.

Spread Your Wealth

Never put more than $100,000 in one bank. Even then, you should make sure the bank you're with is U.S. government insured for $100,000.

Diversify Your Investments

Gold and silver bullion, personally held, is best. Buy secured bonds only. Consider things like casino stock or alcohol and cigarette stocks. Human abuses will always increase, unfortunately. The wealth of the wicked is laid up for the just (Prov. 13:22).

Avoid Stock Market Best Performers

Past performance is no guarantee of future performance. It is my opinion that the stock market is run by insider information. Insiders control the value of stocks, and you, as the public, have old information. By the time you recognize a stock as a good performer, the information is already thirty days old. Learn to second guess and anticipate.

> Learn to second guess and anticipate.

Invest in Collectables

Collect old gold and silver coins. Collectable art pieces and diamonds at or below wholesale prices are also great investments. Be
careful, however. There are a lot of fakes out there. This is an area
that requires becoming especially literate. Learn all you can.

Stash Some Cash

Have enough cash put away in your personal possession to cover
three months' expenses.

Study the Federal Reserve System

Understand how it works. There are many problems with the
Federal Reserve System that you should be aware of. The Federal Reserve System is the supreme instrument for money and
it is used to exert considerable control over the economy. It puts
tremendous economic power into the hands of a very few people
who then have the ability to alter interest rates, affect inflation,
generate taxes, and either stabilize or destabilize the economy,
depending on the policies adopted. This system is not subject to
the same kinds of checks and balances that Americans associate with most government activities. Inevitably, this means that
decisions will not be made with the best interest of the public in
mind. That is simply human nature. In fact, it could be argued,
and many have argued, that the Federal Reserve is an instrument moving toward a totalitarian, one-world economy.[1]

While you may not be able to control the decisions of the Federal Reserve, by understanding how it works and what effects it
has on the economy, you can better prepare yourself to predict
trends in the economy and you will be in a position to make more
intelligent investments.

Last, it is important to understand the state of America today.
There are now over seventy million baby boomers who control
trillions of dollars.[2] They are reaching retirement age at an ex-

tremely rapid rate. They will live life to its fullest and, in my opinion, they will spend their money.

Knowing this, you should look for investments that cater to anti-aging and retirement properties. The top 1 percent are working diligently to get this money. A number of things can affect where this money goes. Forced early retirement, for example, produces a devaluation of the

> Understand the state of America today.

profits on 401(k) plans. Jeopardizing Social Security benefits increases medical costs. Raising or lowering stock prices on the Dow Jones and NASDAQ sucks up investments. Rising interest rates devalue homes that the boomers were planning to sell for a profit. All of these things eat into the trillions of dollars controlled by the baby boomers.

What this means for you is that all you have to do is second guess where that money will be spent and focus your investment strategy accordingly. For example, you should look at retirement properties on or near lakes or mountains with moderate temperatures, little maintenance, and close to gambling, shopping, fishing, skiing, and boating. Log cabins are part of the heart of the baby boomers' nostalgia. Borrow 49 percent of your 401(k) plan and invest in these properties. If you are wise, you'll make more money than the brokers who invest your 401(k) ever will.

You should also consider that 401(k) plans are on the way out. IRAs give you more personal control. Also consider real estate trusts, which now guarantee 7 percent or more on your money.

These are just a few of the things you can begin to do right away. The money is out there. You don't have to settle for just getting by, but you have to gain knowledge and understanding, and you have to act. Become financially literate and develop your skills, and the share of the wealth that God wants you to have will come to you.

Chapter 14 Summary

Becoming Financially Literate

You should be aware of four basic points:

1. God wants you to be prosperous.
2. You have to do something—invest—if you want to be prosperous.
3. If you invest God's way, He will multiply your efforts.
4. You must become financially literate before you begin investing.

Here are some things you can do now, to become financially literate:

- **Reduce real debt:** If it's worth more than you owe, it's an asset. If its value is so low that you would lose money selling it, it is considered "real debt" and should be avoided.
- **Spread your wealth:** Never put more than $100,000 in one bank. Make sure the bank you're with is U.S. government insured for $100,000.
- **Diversify your investments:** Consider things like casino stock or alcohol and cigarette stocks. The wealth of the wicked is laid up for the just (Prov. 13:22).
- **Avoid stock market best performers:** Past performance is no guarantee of future performance. Learn to second guess and anticipate.

- **Invest in collectables:** Coins, art pieces, and diamonds at or below wholesale prices are great investments.
- **Stash some cash:** Have enough cash put away in your personal possession to cover three months' expenses.
- **Study the Federal Reserve System:** By understanding how it works and what effects it has on the economy, you can better prepare yourself to predict trends in the economy and you will be in a position to make more intelligent investments.

Conclusion, but Not the End

We have reached the end of this book, but it is only the beginning of your prosperity. God wants your finances to multiply. This multiplication is yours if you will become financially literate and begin applying biblical truth now.

The principles are not difficult, but it is amazing how few people in the church grasp them. Bible education is crucial to your life. In no way does what I am saying detract from that fact. You need to know the Word and apply it to your life. But secular education is important also. Without it, we will never understand how the finances of the world work, and without understanding that, we will never see the wealth of the world exchanged into the kingdom of God.

Paul was educated in both the Roman culture (the world's ways) and the Hebrew culture (Bible ways). His writings are classic examples of the Greek rhetorical style of presenting arguments. He understood the patterns of literature of the time. In Acts 17, we see Paul in Athens, speaking to a group of religious philosophers. In the course of his comments, he quoted twice from pagan poets. He was familiar with the non-

Christian writings of the time. Paul understood the world around him and how it worked. He used that knowledge to accomplish the destiny God gave him. He had to know the world system to say the things he did to the church in Corinth.

For though I am free from all men, I have made myself a servant to all, that I might win the more; and to the Jews I became as a Jew, that I might win Jews; to those who are under the law, as under the law, that I might win those who are under the law; to those who are without law, as without law (not being without law toward God, but under law toward Christ), that I might win those who are without law; to the weak I became as weak, that I might win the weak, I have become all things to all men, that I might by all means save some. (1 Cor. 9:19–23)

Jesus was one-hundred percent God and one-hundred percent man. He understood both the world system and Scripture. When you examine the organization of Jesus' ministry, you will see that He followed sound principles of business. He set up a base of operations in Capernaum. The evidence suggests that He had His own house that He worked out of. He had wealthy people who supported His ministry financially. He was wealthy Himself.

Jesus approached His task in an intelligent and logical fashion, meaning that He didn't just take off and preach anywhere He happened to end up. He methodically covered all of Galilee for two and a half years. During that time, He put together an administrative organization that developed leaders (the disciples) and had specific offices filled by specific people who were trained for the job. There was even a treasurer (Judas) who handled the organization's money. With the structure of a sound business organization in operation, Jesus moved to the region of Perea, where He was able to accomplish the same things in six months instead of two and a half years. With a multiplied number of disciples and an expanded administrative structure, He moved on to

Judea, which was evangelized in three months. Jesus understood how the business of the ministry works. He understood both the Word and the world.

The church has generally ignored the principles by which wealth operates and instead focused on being spiritual. As a result, it is safe to say that the world has understood the principles of business and investment far better than the church. Jesus said that the children of the world were wiser than God's children (Luk. 16:8). The context of that verse is the Parable of the Unjust Steward. Jesus did not mean that this was how it should be. He was pointing out that this was the way it was but it needed to be changed.

The irony of it all is that the principles the world uses to gain wealth were in the Word of God all the time. That's where they came from. The truths of how to obtain wealth are not worldly principles at all; they are God's principles for obtaining and managing money. This makes it all the more tragic that Christians have shunned them for so long in the interests of spirituality. It is time we realize that becoming financially literate and wisely handling the wealth that God has entrusted to us is as spiritual as prayer and Bible study. It is an essential part of building the kingdom of God.

> The principles the world uses to gain wealth were in the Word of God all the time.

In this book, I have presented the basic steps necessary for you to get to where God wants His people to be. If you have understood them, you will begin to make changes in your life that will lead you to success. Finishing this book is not the end of your search for prosperity. It is the beginning of a way of life that will make you highly influential in the kingdom of God.

Step one is the reconciliation of man to God through Jesus. Salvation begins with the belief that Jesus died for the sins of all mankind, rose from the grave, and now offers new life to any who will receive it. If you have never experienced this new relationship with God, you can do so by simply asking Jesus to forgive your sins and come into your life. It is the beginning of new life.

But salvation, as the Bible describes it, is so much more. Jesus told Zacchaeus that the Son of Man had come to seek and to save "that" which was lost, not just "those" who were lost. His goal is to place man in the original state that Adam was in. Jesus became the second Adam so that He could reconcile the whole earth to Himself. He is interested in saving our finances too. Salvation involves moving into the freedom of prosperity that God planned for His people.

Step two is to understand that it is God's will for His people to have wealth. It was all created by God anyway, and He did not create it for someone else to use. He created it for His kids. You need to grasp this concept fully. Many of the religious people you know will try their best to convince you that God wants you to be sick and poor and ignorant. You need to be able to answer

> It is God's will for His people to have wealth.

them with an understanding of the Word: "For we do not commend ourselves again to you, but give you opportunity to boast on our behalf, that you may have an answer for those who boast in appearance and not in heart" (2 Cor. 5:12).

Step three is recognizing that man's purpose on this earth was and is summed up in Genesis 1:26–28—to be fruitful, multiply, and fill the earth. Man was created to produce, to build business, and to multiply money into great wealth. To fulfill your purpose means to create an inheritance for your children's children, to love God, and to represent Him to the world (Prov. 13:22).

Man was also created to have dominion over the earth. The church has abdicated that authority in many areas that have become dark and ungodly such as education, television, radio,

politics, medicine, and the judicial system. It is absolutely critical that Christians begin to reclaim those areas in order to
straighten them out. We can't do the job without money. It takes
money to put together educational programs that can affect our
children and our schools. It takes money to create and air television and radio programs that are healthy for our families. It
takes money to run for political office. Gaining wealth is essential for the fulfillment of our calling to have dominion. If we turn
our backs on it in an attempt to be spiritual, our whole society
will crumble.

Step four is actually becoming financially literate. We can
begin by learning to understand the process of loss and gain.
Worldwide, during the nineteenth and twentieth centuries, we
developed from a rural to an industrial society. As rural dwellers,
we followed a program that was consistent with the way crops
grew. We planted seed, watered it, and harvested or received the
crop. We would take of the first fruit, the first ten percent, and
we would tithe to the storehouse. This would be followed by an
offering of the next best seed, also into the storehouse. Out of the
strongest seed left over after the tithes and offerings, ten percent
was set aside to replant in the spring for another harvest. We ate
what was left.

The tithes and the offerings were insurance that what we had
would not be lost. God said that when we tithed He would rebuke
the devourer on our behalf (Mal. 3:10–11). In other words, God
said, "Bring the whole tithe and offering, all of it, into the storehouse and I will protect the other seed that you plant in the earth.
Your trees will not be lost and the pest will not eat your crops."

The offering caused the windows of heaven to open so that
God could pour out so much harvest that we could not contain
it. It brought blessing on the seed we planted for the next harvest.
Of course, if we did not plant the seed, then there was nothing to
bless. But the seed planted in those circumstances would produce
thirty, sixty, and a hundredfold return.

As we became an industrial society, we lost track of part of the process. Debt and the deceitfulness of riches (Mrk. 4:19) have kept us working for money rather than having money work for us. We no longer directly handle the actual seed or harvest. Instead, we now deal with money in a much more abstract way. We began to lose sight of the principles of sowing and harvesting that every farmer should know. We have lost track of the multiplication stage. Instead of multiplying our seed and harvesting thirty, sixty, and a hundredfold, we have remained in the stage of unfruitfulness.

We must understand the process of multiplication. We must do the same things with our money that we used to do with seed. The first fruits, the ten percent, need to be tithed into the storehouse, the church where you are a member, so that God can protect you from the attacks of the devourer. If you don't belong to a church, then

> We must do the same things with our money that we used to do with seed.

you need to get into one. In addition to the tithe, there need to be offerings, also into the storehouse, so that the windows of heaven can open and blessing can come to your investments.

Many Christians today have figured out this much but they have not learned to invest so that God has something to bless. The next ten percent needs to be invested. Because we are used to eating the rest of our seed, we have nothing left to invest in tomorrow's harvest. When we connect our faith to the investment, God can multiply the seed so that everything your hand touches will prosper. He gives the ability to produce a harvest of thirty, sixty, and a hundredfold (Mrk. 4:20) because we hear the Word and receive it.

Step five is beginning the process of no longer working for money but making money work for us. If we are working for money, then we are slaves to it.

No one can serve two masters; for either he will hate the one and love the other, or else he will be loyal to the one and despise the other. You cannot serve God and mammon. (Matt. 6:24)

We all start out working to make money. But we must not stop there. We must advance to the position that money serves us so that we can devote our time to serving God and not being controlled by the need to make money to survive. We need to have enough determination and passion to drive us to do whatever it takes to become financially literate and get control of our finances.

Steps four and five include a great deal of study. Financial literacy is absolutely essential. Don't invest in the stock market until you know something about the stock market. Don't buy a lot of real estate until you understand real estate. There are some risks in any investment, but you can minimize those risks by using your brain. Once you have gained a working knowledge of the areas of investment you are ready to begin.

> Financial literacy is absolutely essential. Don't invest in the stock market until you know something about the stock market.

Give your tithe. Give your offering. Then invest at least ten percent of your income in real estate, stocks, and bonds. Learn to buy low and sell high, just as Joseph did. When there was a surplus in Genesis 41, he bought low. In chapter 47 there was a shortage and he sold high, amassing tremendous wealth.

The parable of the *minas* in Luke 19:11–27 shows us a picture of Jesus coming and giving seed to the sower in the productive stage. The king, who I believe represents Jesus, gave each of ten servants one *mina* and told them to "do business" until he came back. One traded and invested and turned his one *mina* into ten.

Another multiplied his *mina* five times. A third servant did nothing with the money but hide it.

When Jesus returned, these three were the only ones of the ten servants that even showed up. He called the one who had multiplied his investment ten times and said to him, "Well done, good and faithful servant. Because you were faithful in a little, I will make you ruler over much." When the second servant showed that he had multiplied his *mina* five times, Jesus said, "Well done, good and faithful servant. Because you were faithful in a little, I will make you ruler over much." Jesus called the one who did nothing with his money a wicked and evil servant.

What qualified the first two servants to be good and faithful was the fact that they had taken their money and invested it so that it multiplied. Note that the only time Jesus calls us good and faithful servants is when we are in the multiplying stage for the sake of the kingdom and we are making money work for us. Multiplying money for the sake of the kingdom is what good and faithful servants do. When we see these matters in the right perspective, we begin to work for the kingdom without concern for

> The only time Jesus calls us good and faithful servants is when we are in the multiplying stage.

money. The money to accomplish our destiny is always available because the wealth of the wicked is stored up for the just, and it is just about time we get to it!

Notes

Chapter 3. Light a Fire

1. James Strong, *Strong's Exhaustive Concordance of The Bible* (Peabody, Massachusetts: Hendrickson Publishers, 2007).
2. Ibid.

Chapter 6. You're Brain-Dead

1. John H. Munroe, "The Economic History of Modern Europe to 1914" (lecture, University of Toronto, Toronto, Ontario, September 11, 2007).
2. Deb and Pam Holice, *The History of New York State*, ed. Dr. James Sullivan (Lewis Historical Publishing Company, Inc., 1927); http://www.usgennet.org/usa/ny/state/his.
3. *Online Etymology Dictionary*, s.v. "broker," http://www.etymonline.com/index.php?term=broker.

Chapter 10. Bulldog Tenacity

1. The History Place, "Abraham Lincoln," http://www.historyplace.com/lincoln.

Chapter 13. Jesus Wasn't Poor

1. James Strong, *Strong's Exhaustive Concordance of The Bible* (Peabody, Massachusetts: Hendrickson Publishers, 2007).
2. Ibid.
3. Ibid.
4. Ibid.

Chapter 14. Becoming Financially Literate

1. G. Edward Griffin, The Creature from Jekyll Island: A Second Look at the Federal Reserve (Southern California: American Media, 2002).
2. Wikipedia, s.v. "baby boomers," http://en.wikipedia.org/wiki/baby_boomer.

About the Author

AFTER GROWING UP IN A SHACK IN LORETTA, WISCONSIN, DR. ANDER-
son knows what it is like to struggle financially. In *Becoming a
Millionaire God's Way*, he shares the principles learned through
diligence, hard work, and personal experience that brought him
from poverty to abundance. Dr. C. Thomas Anderson is the senior
pastor and founder of Living Word Bible Church in Mesa, Arizona. With over 8,500 members, Living Word is the largest Word
of Faith church in Arizona. With over thirty years of experience in
ministering the Gospel, he continues to travel the world leaving
a mark that can never be erased. His humor, motivational ability,
and anointed messages place him in great demand.